WHAT GREAT SALESPEOPLE DO

WHAT GREAT SALESPEOPLE DO

The Science of Selling Through Emotional Connection and the Power of Story

MICHAEL BOSWORTH
BEN ZOLDAN

New York Chicago San Francisco Lisbon London Madrid Mexico City
Milan New Delhi San Juan Seoul Singapore Sydney Toronto

6 7 8 9 0 QFR/QFR 1 6 5

ISBN 978-0-07-176971-6
MHID 0-07-176971-4

e-ISBN 978-0-07-176974-7
e-MHID 0-07-176974-9

This publication is designed to provide accurate and authoritative information in regard to the subject matter covered. It is sold with the understanding that neither the authors nor the publisher are engaged in rendering legal, accounting, securities trading, or other professional service. If legal advice or other expert assistance is required, the services of a competent professional person should be sought.

> —From a Declaration of Principles Jointly Adopted by a Committee of the American Bar Association and a Committee of Publishers and Associations

McGraw-Hill books are available at special quantity discounts to use as premiums and sales promotions or for use in corporate training programs. To contact a representative, please e-mail us at bulksales@mcgraw-hill.com.

CONTENTS

APPRECIATION

We would like to thank the following people for making this book possible.

From Mike:
My grandmother, Genevieve Bosworth, and my sister, Leslie Bosworth Schuler, the most influential storytellers during my first 30 years. My whole extended Bosworth clan, for their love and support; my children, Brendan, Brian, and Shiloah; my emotional support group of Judy, Jean, Madeline, Rosy, Gina, and Julie; my intellectual support group of Charles, Dave, Ron, and Kevin; my sales role model, Jim Campbell; my wonderful life partner, Jennifer Lehr; and most of all, my creative and courageous partner and coauthor, Ben Zoldan. Ben's courage in leaving his comfort zone has been an inspiration to me, and collaborating with him has been tons of fun!

From Ben:
My loving and supportive wife, Tia, and our two beautiful daughters, Zoe and Abby—I cannot get enough of their stories; my entire family and my close circle of friends; Mark Sage, L.M.F.T., a true role model (especially for role modeling real empathy); and my coauthor of this book and cofounder of our Story Leaders business, Mike, whom I have

known for more than 15 years. Mike has been a mentor, friend, and is family to me.

From the both of us:

Will Allison, our collaborator on this book project, who through his empathic listening helped bring our voice to the page.

John Burke, the best Story Leader we know, an inspiration to us both, someone who challenges the status quo.

Phil Godwin, for having the vision to take a leap of faith and bring Story Leaders into his business and for being a blast to work with.

Tom Albers, an innovative software executive who supported our efforts to launch Story Leaders, LLC.

And finally, all the people mentioned in this book, from the stories you shared with us, to the research you provided— we are so appreciative!

—**Mike and Ben**

INTRODUCTION

Ben's Story: Zoe's History Lesson

Before we get into what great salespeople do, I'd like to share a story about my daughter Zoe, one that brought new meaning to the work Mike and I are doing.

Last January, my wife and I attended a midyear parent-teacher conference. Zoe was in sixth grade, and we were expecting the usual—a glowing report. But this meeting was different. I could tell there was a problem from the moment we sat down with Zoe's teacher.

"Zoe is struggling in history," she said. She explained that Zoe's test scores had dropped. Maybe it was Zoe's comprehension, or maybe it was her recall—the teacher couldn't be sure. The news hit me like a punch in the stomach. Something was wrong with my little girl, and the teacher couldn't even tell me what it was. On top of that, I'd always loved history, and I wanted it to be a subject my kids loved, too.

That night, I asked Zoe about history. She said she hated having to remember stupid names, dates, and facts. "Why do I need to know what happened to a bunch of old men 200 years ago?" she asked.

They'd just finished studying colonial American history, so I asked her what she'd learned about the Revolution.

"They signed the Declaration of Independence," she said.

"What did that mean?"

"I don't remember," she said.

Over the next few weeks, I asked some of Zoe's friends about history, and they all felt the same way she did. I just didn't get it. I remembered history lessons as being full of exciting stories about interesting people. To this day, I still remember learning about Paul Revere in grade school.

Paul was born to a French immigrant father who came to the new colonies when he was 13. Paul's mother was a New England socialite from an established Boston area family. As a young boy, Paul loved working as an apprentice to his father, a silversmith. His dad was known as the best engraver around, and Paul wanted to be just like him. He instilled in Paul an entrepreneurial ethic: "Make something of yourself."

Paul also greatly admired his mother and her community activism. The family went to church every Sunday and discussed politics, business, and religion at dinner every night. No subject was out of bounds. Paul soon began to form his own views on important subjects of the day, particularly the Church of England.

When Paul was 17, his father died. Paul was doubly crushed. He wanted to take over the silversmith business, but according to English law, he was too young. With few options, he enlisted in the Provincial Army to fight in the French and Indian War. During the war, Paul experienced tyranny and oppression firsthand. He emerged from the army an independent thinker who was not afraid to challenge the status quo and fight for what he believed was right.

Because I connected with Paul's story, I never had any trouble understanding and remembering the related historic events: the Boston Tea Party, the colonies voting to reject British rule and adopt the Declaration of Independence, the "shot heard around the world," and of course Paul's famous ride ("The British are coming, the British are coming!"). But when I tried telling Zoe the story, hoping to spark her interest, she just gave me a funny look.

"Dad," she said, "that's not how we learn history."

That's when I remembered seeing the new Smart Board in her classroom during the parent-teacher conference. Smart Boards are "interactive whiteboards" that have begun replacing traditional chalkboards in a lot of American classrooms, and all of the classes in Zoe's school had gotten them at the beginning of the year. Among other things, Smart Boards allow teachers to present their lessons in the form of PowerPoint presentations. Figure I.1 on the following page shows the PowerPoint slide Zoe's teacher used in her lesson about the Declaration of Independence.

You can see the difference between the ways Zoe and I learned history: All she got was *what* happened. I got the *what* **and** the *why*. Of course, Zoe isn't the only student to suffer this sort of "teaching," and the problem isn't confined to our educational system. The same thing is happening every day in corporate America. We try to educate our salespeople by burying them in an avalanche of facts and figures. Then they go out into the field and do the same thing to customers. It's little surprise so few of those customers buy in. They don't like it any more than Zoe did.

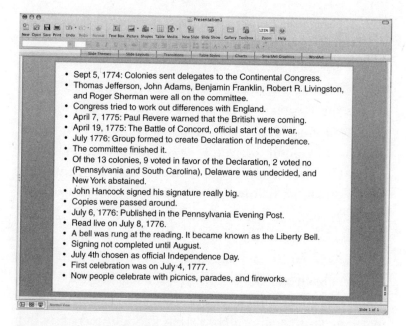

Figure I.1 The PowerPoint Slide Zoe's Teacher Used in Her Lesson About the Declaration of Independence

Why Did We Write This Book?

We set out to demystify *what great salespeople do.*

We began this journey primarily for ourselves, to improve how we sell. Sales is the only career the two of us have ever known. And we wrote this book to share what we've discovered along this journey—how we can all better influence change in the world.

Here's what we have always known about selling:

People decide *who* to buy from as much as *what* to buy.
People prefer to do business with people like themselves.
Selling is a social endeavor involving interpersonal relationships.

A person's effectiveness as a communicator has a direct
impact on his or her effectiveness selling.

The best salespeople communicate in a way that gets
people to share information about themselves; fosters
openness to new ideas; and inspires others to take
action (i.e., to buy).

What we *didn't* know was what makes the best salespeople such effective communicators. Was it personality,
intelligence, persistence, experience, background, or just
plain luck? Was it an inherent gift, or could it be learned
and taught?

We've been training salespeople for a combined 40 years.
For most of that time, our definition of selling has been some
variation of "helping people solve problems." The definition was based on the belief that the decision to "buy" is like
problem solving, logical and rational.

At the time we got into the sales enablement industry,
empirical industry research had established that what distin-
guished successful sellers from less successful ones was questions: the best sellers asked their customers questions. Lots of
questions. So for our Solution Selling and CustomerCentric
Selling workshops, we taught salespeople to ask buyers a
series of logic-oriented questions designed to lead the buyer
to conclude the seller's product was the logical, *right* answer.

As it turns out, a lot of our basic assumptions were wrong.
People are not logical and rational when making the decision to buy. Furthermore, asking buyers questions—at least
the kinds of questions we were training salespeople to ask—
is not an effective means of connection or persuasion. In
fact, the way we conditioned salespeople to ask questions
has proven to be often counterproductive.

It also turns out that a lot of the early sales industry research had misinterpreted what the most influential salespeople were actually doing. They weren't just asking buyers questions; they were establishing emotional connections, building what we used to call "rapport." They were doing things that weren't being taught in our training or anyone else's.

In the introduction to his bestselling book *Solution Selling* (1994), Mike wrote, "Superior sellers (I call them Eagles) have intuitive relationship building skills; they empathically listen, they establish sincerity early in the sales call, and they establish a high level of confidence with their buyer." These skills—relationship building, empathic listening, and so forth—were not addressed any further in the book because, frankly, we didn't know what else to say about it. To our knowledge, they weren't teachable skills. Either you had the gift or you didn't.

Nearly two decades after the publication of *Solution Selling*, the sales profession hasn't changed much. Other professions have evolved and moved forward, but we're still doing things the same way we did 20 years ago, and it's still not working.

When we first began training salespeople, we used to talk about the "80/20 rule": in most companies, 20 percent of the salespeople brought in 80 percent of the business, while the other 80 percent of salespeople fought over the scraps. Only a few salespeople were able to develop mutual trust and respect with customers. Only a few were able to reach the high level of connection that fosters collaboration, the reciprocal sharing of ideas and beliefs that can move people to change.

If the prevailing sales models worked, you'd expect a shift away from the 80/20 rule over the years as more sellers improved and took a bigger slice of the pie. In fact, it's gotten worse. Recent research shows that the gap between the best sellers and the rest of the pack has actually widened. This is an especially hard pill for us to swallow, because we're the ones who created the paradigm.

So why aren't we as a profession getting better at what we do? What's holding us back? And why haven't we been pursuing these questions more aggressively? It's ironic: somewhere along the line, a profession whose prevailing model is based on questions stopped asking questions about itself.

So we did it. We began challenging our own beliefs, starting with, "Is there a better way?" This led to more and more questions, a domino effect, and soon we found ourselves in fields of study that had been previously off limits to us—fields that explored the mysteries of communication that we'd written off as unteachable because they fell outside the purview of our models and industry research.

What we soon learned was that we should have been looking for answers outside the sales productivity industry all along. People in other disciplines already understood a lot more about sales than professional salespeople did. Our research led us to an entirely new definition of selling. Selling isn't about "solving problems" or "providing solutions." Selling is *influencing change*—influencing people to change. This definition is based on a greater understanding of how we decide to trust some people and not others, how we decide to take a leap of faith and try something new, how we decide to buy or not to buy.

In this book, we share our stories and our findings, drawing on our decades of personal selling experience and synthesizing research from a wide range of disciplines including neuroscience, psychology, sociology, anthropology, and others. We pull it all together into a field-tested framework developed in our Story Leaders workshops. It's a book for sales professionals and for anyone else—executives, politicians, teachers, attorneys, consultants, parents, and so on—whose work involves influencing others, whether you're "selling" products, services, ideas, advice, or beliefs.

By demystifying *what great salespeople do*, we believe we ourselves have learned to better influence change, develop deeper relationships with our customers, and find greater meaning in selling.

CHAPTER 1

The Old Paradigm

> It is not the strongest of the species that survive, nor the most intelligent, but the one most responsive to change.
> —Charles Darwin

Ben's Story: John Scanlon

It was early 2008, and I was teaching a CustomerCentric Selling workshop to a longtime client. During the workshop, one of the students, Jason, asked if I'd like to sit in on a sales call he had scheduled for the afternoon immediately following the class.

By this point, I had worked with this company for a while, and I had trained virtually everyone in the organization—everyone except one key person, the CEO John Scanlon.

On Friday afternoon, having just finished the class, Jason and I headed to a conference room down the hall for the sales call. The prospect, a CIO, was there with two of his IT directors, plus an unexpected fourth person: John Scanlon, my client's CEO. I quickly realized it would be a great opportunity to showcase our methodology to someone who'd always been too busy to come to the workshop. The sales call began with Jason doing everything he'd just learned. He opened with an agenda, gave a quick overview of his company, and within the first two minutes transitioned into his diagnostic questions in an attempt to get the buyer to open up about his situation.

The prospect, however, didn't respond the way that he was supposed to. Although Jason's questions were straight from the "playbook," the CIO's answers became increasingly abrupt. Soon he was down to one-word answers. Worse, his body language—arms crossed, stiff posture, zero eye contact—was registering what could best be described as irritation.

Within minutes, the call flipped: Jason was no longer the one asking the questions. The CIO had taken over the interrogation, and Jason was responding by talking about *what* his products do, the very thing we try to avoid early in a conversation. I couldn't help myself. I jumped in to try to get things back on track. I asked the CIO what I thought was a perfectly reasonable question about his current environment. I can't remember exactly what I said, but I do remember the CIO getting upset and cutting me short.

"Stop!" he said. "You're not getting me. Stop asking me so many questions and tell me what you do."

Ten seconds in, I had crashed and burned along with Jason. I looked over at John, the CEO, and could only imagine what he was thinking: "*This* is what we're training our salespeople to do?"

After a few seconds of very uncomfortable silence, John, who had been quiet this whole time, leaned forward and, in a calming, soft voice, said, "Hey guys, this reminds me of a time when I was at MCI . . ." And he began to tell a story about when he used to work for MCI and the chaos that resulted after a merger. He very specifically described how he and his management team had made a series of mistakes that led to a series of customer problems. As John was telling his story, the feeling in the room immediately began to change: the CIO began to relax. He uncrossed his arms. He set aside his BlackBerry, which had been consuming his attention, and leaned toward John. John ended his story with, "What I learned from that experience was . . ." The story lasted no more than three minutes, and when he was finished, John fell silent. He didn't prompt anyone else to speak, and he didn't ask any questions. I had no idea what to do at that point. I could think of nothing to add. Neither could Jason.

After only a few seconds, the once-tense CIO said, "You know, John, I was a client of MCI at the same time, and here is what I went through . . ." And then he launched into a related story about a similar experience. And John listened—really *listened*.

When the CIO was done with his story, the room got quiet again. Then John started another story, but this one was more personal. It included his kids and was only marginally relevant to the conversation. The CIO then offered a story about *his* kids, plus his in-laws. This went on for probably another 30 minutes, with John and the CIO alternating between personal, business, and company stories. And then, about 45 minutes into the meeting, the CIO said, "Here's the thing, John; we're on three continents. Can you support us on all three continents?"

John gave the question some thought. "I have no idea," he said. "We've never done this before."

I looked over at Jason and could tell he wanted to strangle John. We were thinking the same thing: *No! You can't say that to a prospect!*

"But I am in this together with you," John added.

The room fell silent again as Jason and I sat there in disbelief. Finally, the CIO turned to his two IT directors. "Okay," he said. "What do we need to do to get started?"

The three of them talked it over, and then the CIO turned back to John and gave him the green light to move forward. The meeting was effectively over, the deal closed, and the details to be worked out later.

As John and the clients left the room, making friendly small talk, I was left sitting there in silence with Jason, both of us wondering, "What just happened?"

Decoding the "John Method"

Although the sales call was a "success," I left feeling deflated. I'd flopped and so had the person I'd just trained. I'd had plenty of my own unsuccessful sales calls in the past, but this was different. This one was supposed to showcase the methodology, but it hadn't.

At first, I wasn't able to make sense of what John had done. When I got to the airport, I went straight to the lounge, ordered a drink, and tried to decode what I had watched John do. On a cocktail napkin, I wrote down a list of words that reflected what I thought I saw in John:

Vulnerable
Caring
Authentic
Listened
Storyteller

4

I sat there staring at the list, trying to get my head around what it all meant.

John had shared real stories—some professional, some personal—but in all cases, they were unlike any stories I'd ever heard before in a sales meeting. He was vulnerable; all of his stories included some admission of his own mistakes, which seemed crazy to me at the time. Even as the CEO, he didn't try to come across as Superman; he just seemed human. He had a point to every story he told, though I wouldn't realize this until later. He was patient and demonstrated empathic listening—real listening beyond anything I'd known was possible. He seemed to really care. Ultimately, he somehow got the CIO to reveal everything that Jason would have wanted him to reveal: his challenges, his goals, his personal experiences, his beliefs.

But the kicker was what John *didn't* do. He never asked a single question. Not even one. And yet he was able to get the guarded, arms-crossed CIO to completely open up and reveal himself.

Later, when I asked other people about John, the response was always, "He just puts people at ease. He has all the intangibles." Nobody could explain what those intangibles were, nor was anyone teaching the "John method." Everything John did seemed to work, and it looked so simple. He was a better salesperson than anyone in his sales force—the people I had trained. What did that say about our sales training?

When I tell people this story now, some say, "John had an advantage because he is the CEO." My question is, "Was John able to sell that way because he was the CEO, or was he the CEO because he could sell that way?"

We Didn't Take This Stuff Seriously

The next day, I drove to the bookstore near my house, went straight to the business section, and found the sales shelf. I'd brought my napkin with the list of words. I started going through all the sales books, including ours, *CustomerCentric Selling*. I wasn't able to find a single one that included a meaningful discussion of authenticity, vulnerability, listening, or storytelling.

To my left were the psychology and relationships sections. On a hunch, I started going through those books too. This time, I found a wealth of content that explained the qualities John had demonstrated—books about listening, caring, empathy, authenticity, vulnerability, story sharing, emotions, connecting, and relationships.

Next to the psychology section was the medical reference section. I looked at those books as well. They dovetailed with the psychology and relationship books in their emphasis on new brain science and neurobiology. I was finding that all of these disciplines built upon each other, and that they all took human behavior and relationships much more seriously than we did in the sales training world. *These* were the books that were teaching the "John method." That's right—there were better sales training books in the psychology and medical reference sections than in the business section.

Mike's Story: 87/13

In many ways, it was just another annual affiliate meeting, similar to the dozens I had hosted in the past. As I sat down in the conference room with our CustomerCentric Selling affiliates, I was looking forward to an inspirational annual kickoff event. I was surrounded by my friends, colleagues, and disciples, all of whom shared a belief in our methodology.

More important, I truly felt, at the time, that I was achieving my goal to help the vast majority of sales professionals to become better at their craft. Decades ago, Xerox found that the top 20 percent of its sales force was responsible for 80 percent of the sales revenue, while the other 80 percent struggled to make the remaining 20 percent of the revenue. I believed, with all my heart, that both the Solution Selling and CustomerCentric Selling methodologies held the key to helping the bottom 80 percent.

The meeting began as all such meeting do, with everyone settled in and ready to hear something new. One of my partners had hired a sales industry researcher to be the keynote speaker. As he started his presentation, Greg Alexander, founder of Sales Benchmark Index, put up a slide with two numbers on it: 87 and 13. He told us that the 80/20 rule was no longer true. Instead, in business-to-business (B2B) sales, after indexing 1,100 B2B sales organizations—including many of our clients who employed thousands of salespeople we had trained—he'd found that the ratio was now 87/13. The top 13 percent of salespeople were now responsible for 87 percent of the revenue.

I stared at the slide. The net effect of decades of sales training hadn't helped the great mass of salespeople. Instead, systems like Solution Selling and CustomerCentric Selling had made the best salespeople even better, leaving their peers even further behind. A few days later, it really hit me. Despite my best intentions, I hadn't accomplished what I set out to do—help the bottom 80 percent pay their mortgages, send their kids to college, take vacations, and provide for their families. I realized that my confidence in our methodology had turned into intellectual arrogance.

At first, I tried to cram that uncomfortable realization back into the bottle. The 87 percent must be lazy, stubborn, or resistant to change, I told myself. If they really tried, they could learn how to do it. After all, it had worked for me. And I thought I had evidence that our training wasn't the problem. The number-one complaint I heard from sales managers was that the bottom 80 percent of their salespeople quit trying to use the methodology within 10 days of the workshop, whereas the top people had an easy time putting the methodology into practice and therefore stuck with it. It stood to reason that the few top sellers were successful because they used our methodology, while the rest underperformed because they didn't.

At CustomerCentric Selling, we prided ourselves on using our methodology to sell our methodology, so I took out a pad and ran the numbers, hoping to prove myself right. No such luck. Of approximately 40 affiliates, five of them had brought in 90 percent of our revenue—and it was the same five people every year. In theory, if all 40 were using our methodology, the revenue spread would have been a lot less disproportionate. But the real "aha moment" wasn't that 87/13 was alive and well within my own organization. That moment came a little later when I looked under the hood at those top five affiliates and considered what set them apart from the others. And there it was: they were the ones who had what we used to call "the mojo," the ability to forge real emotional connections with their customers. They weren't necessarily using the methodology they were selling. They were doing something different—more like what John did.

Ben's Story: Learning from the Inside Out

Ever since the John Scanlon experience, and even more so after our affiliate meeting, Mike and I had committed ourselves to learning more. We'd been immersed in research, from psychology to interpersonal relationships and even the neurosciences, studying subjects previously way outside our realm. The more we read, the clearer it became that our sales model—the one we'd been teaching all those years; the one we believed in—was badly flawed. We'd wildly misunderstood what made great salespeople great. We'd given it our best shot, based on what we knew at the time, but we still hadn't cracked the code on what the best were doing.

Now, piece by piece, without quite meaning to, we began to develop a new approach, one that drew on other disciplines and on new scientific knowledge. Our research became more intense. We moved away from a logic-oriented model and began to focus on emotional intelligence and the power of connection. The answers lay in the neurosciences and psychology. We were learning about the brain and the mind—how it works, the neurological sources of feelings such as empathy, and recent discoveries that have reshaped our understanding of how and why people change. This was light years ahead of what was happening in the sales training departments of corporate America.

Along the way, we realized that John Scanlon wasn't the only one who embodied our new understanding of influence. Now that our eyes were open, we saw it over and over again in all the other top salespeople we knew, the same innate qualities that John had exhibited.

But the big question for us was: were they really innate qualities or could they be learned? By that point, Mike and

I couldn't turn back. It would have been a copout to accept the old explanation: "He just puts people at ease. He has all the intangibles." We set out to deconstruct and codify those intangibles.

My wife was more than a little skeptical.

"You're going to teach *what*?" she said. "What do *you* know about connectedness and vulnerability?"

My first reaction was to ignore her, but she was right. At that point, I had only an intellectual grasp of the material I'd been studying. For proof, I needed to look no further than my own personal relationships. I could talk about vulnerability, but I had not yet learned how to really open up and be vulnerable. I could talk about emotional connectedness, but I'd never connected with a client as effortlessly as John seemed to do. On top of it all, I'd hit a rocky spot in some of my most important personal relationships.

Fast-forward one month. I was now in therapy. But even though I showed up every week, I really wasn't interested in delving into the events of my past. I resisted. The therapy seemed as big a waste of time as I'd decided it would be from the start.

Luckily, out of guilt and a sense of obligation, I stayed with it. And wouldn't you know, before long I began to develop a deeper, more personal, more profound understanding of emotional connection, one that dovetailed with everything I'd been studying. Through therapy I was learning to look within, to search out my memories and experiences and form stories around them that had meaning. For the first time, I was learning how to use language to express feelings and emotions, to articulate the autobiographical stories that account for who I am. This, in turn, helped me listen more empathetically to other people's stories.

By searching out my own experiences—how I felt and the reasons for those feelings—I became more authentically curious about others. I was learning the John method from the inside out.

In retrospect, it's little wonder I'd been so tied to our old sales methodology. It was a left-brain, logical approach that appealed to me at a time when I was living a left-brain life. It was hard for my ego to let go of what I thought I knew. But now, thanks to this journey inspired by John Scanlon, I finally saw the limitations of our old methodology and became open to the more powerful possibilities of whole-brain selling.

And as it happened, Mike and I found ourselves on very similar paths—in our discontent with the old model, in examining our own personal experiences, and now in our shared belief that we could and should go to a place that had been so off-limits to us before. We also both realized we had to experience these new ideas from the inside out, addressing our own struggles first before we could begin to think about teaching others.

CHAPTER 2

Earth Is No Longer the Center of the Universe

> There is only one thing more powerful than all the armies in the world; that is an idea whose time has come.
>
> —Victor Hugo

The Geocentric Model

Understanding how we decide to act is really a story of technology. Technology changes paradigms. People once believed Earth was the center of the universe and all other objects orbited around it. Aristotle's geocentric model served as the predominant cosmological paradigm into the sixteenth century.

There were many good reasons to believe all heavenly bodies circled our planet. The geocentric model was "state of the art" for its time. Astrological observations suggested that the stars, our sun, and all known planets revolved around Earth each day, making Earth the center of that system. The second common notion supporting the geocentric model was that Earth does not seem to move. To an earth-bound observer, our planet appears grounded, solid, stable. What better hypothesis could anyone have come up with, other than Earth was the center of the universe? There was no other explanation.

The first big challenge to the geocentric model came along in the sixteenth century. With the advent of the telescope, Copernicus observed new phenomena, such as instances of moons orbiting other planets. To the majority of people at the time, however, the evidence was not strong enough to change their beliefs.

In 1609, further advancements in technology enabled Galileo to seriously challenge the geocentric paradigm. He was able to see the moons of Jupiter orbiting the planet. However, the evidence was still not great enough to change most people's minds. It took one more year before the tipping point arrived. In that one defining year, as technological advances further improved the telescope, Galileo was able to observe additional planets in orbit around a greater body, just as he had observed with the moons of Jupiter. This was enough evidence to finally dispel the prevailing state-of-the-art model. Through disruptive technology, the world's leading cosmological paradigm was turned on its head: Earth was no longer the center of the universe.

Logic Is No Longer the Center of the Sales Universe

Since ancient civilizations, people have been attempting to understand how our minds work and how we decide to act. Aristotle declared that reason, logic, and rational thought are at the center of our decision-making processes. He believed that emotion wreaks havoc on our otherwise logical behavior.

Other influential thinkers ascribed a more significant role to emotion, but they lacked the technological tools to substantiate their theories. As a result, the realm of emotion, intuition, and "gut feel" went unexplained for centuries. Meanwhile, the paradigm of logic and reason became the basis for the study of influence and persuasion and found its way into twentieth- and early twenty-first-century paradigms of selling.

Just as Aristotle lacked a telescope that could reveal the true nature of the universe, he lacked a "telescope" into the brain that could reveal the true nature of human behavior. Even during most of the twentieth century, the brain was largely a mystery. Since the mid-1990s, however, advances in technology have given scientists the capability to monitor brain processes in real time. With the advent of technologies such as magnetic resonance imaging (MRI), brain scanning, and other digital brain imaging technologies, a new era has emerged in the neurosciences.

Recent observations have completely reshaped our beliefs about what motivates us to act and how we make decisions (e.g., when and how to change and whom to trust) and respond to stimuli. It's a classic case of disruptive new technologies changing a paradigm. We now have a new understanding of influence, persuasion, and selling. We are reminded that Earth is not the center of the universe, and that logic and reason, it turns out, are not at the center of our decision-making processes.

Mike's Story: The "Solution Sale"

When I was first asked to be a sales trainer in 1976 for Xerox Computer Services, my paradigm of selling was based primarily on logic and reason. I defined selling as the process of helping someone solve a problem using our products. At the time, I was the number-one salesperson in the company, and how I "solved someone's problem" was the only way I could explain what differentiated me from the rest of the sales force. I agreed to move into the role of trainer because I saw it as a way to help others.

My paradigm of selling was also shaped by my work with behavioral researcher Neil Rackham in 1979. Revenue production at Xerox, as at most companies, was highly disproportionate, so Xerox hired Rackham to study what the top 20 percent of salespeople were doing so we could teach it to the mediocre masses. This study was called the SPIN project.

Rackham conducted the study by recording the behaviors of both buyers and sellers in 1,500 sales calls made by the top 20 percent of Xerox sellers. We focused on what was observable at the time, given the technology of the time: the types of questions those top sellers were asking.

After poring over the data, all of the people on the SPIN project team, including me, arrived at a linear, logic-oriented, questioning approach. The paradigm held that for a buyer to cooperate with a salesperson, the salesperson had to learn how to ask a series of questions that would lead the buyer to see that the seller's offering was the solution to the buyer's problem. The B2B sales training and productivity industry was born.

Many "variation on a theme" sales methodologies can be traced to the original methodologies—SPIN Selling, Solution Selling, Consultative Selling, CustomerCentric Selling, and so on—all of which were based on helping a buyer use reason and logic to solve a problem, and which include a logic-oriented "value proposition" in order to help a buyer justify a decision. Our global definition of selling was based on the belief that decision making was primarily linear, logical, and rational.

This paradigm discounted the value of emotional connection. At the time, we had no way of even articulating how any two individuals connected emotionally. I had a hunch that people made emotional decisions and then justified those decisions later using logic and value. A basic principle of my early training methodology, Solution Selling, stated: "People make emotional decisions for logical reasons." However, none of us in the industry knew how to explain what an emotional decision really was, much less how to influence one on purpose. The best theory I could muster at the time was that the buyer would want to buy from the seller who created the best vision of using his or her product. Our paradigm of selling was based on the science of the time. We couldn't look inside buyers' and sellers' hearts and minds; all we could do was study their external behaviors and draw our conclusions accordingly. That was the state of the art.

What we didn't focus on during the SPIN project was how the top sellers connected with buyers *before* they started asking their questions. Back then, we used terms like "woo," "mojo," and "gift of gab." However, we had no scientific evidence that something deliberate and replicable was happening. It was just "magic." In fact, Xerox convinced me that emotional connection (what they called "rapport") is the unique chemistry between two people, and no two combinations are the same. I took that as gospel and trusted it for years. I believe the rest of the industry did too. My gut still told me that people make emotional decisions and then support those decisions after the fact with logic. I just had no model to support my gut feeling, no evidence to prove it, so I just didn't deal with it.

And so the old paradigm remained intact. We modeled what we could research and explain. It wasn't until new technologies came along—technologies that allowed us to "see" inside the brain—that we finally had our own version of Galileo's telescope, one that forced us to completely reevaluate our logic-based sales paradigm.

The New Science of the Brain

Technology over the past 15 years has seriously undermined our old understanding of decision making, persuasion, influence, and change. For the first time in history, neuroscientists are able to see into the source of what was previously unexplainable: how our minds actually work.

Breakthroughs in the field of neuroscience have revealed that our decisions are not solely based on logic—not even close. In fact, decision-making processes are much more complex and use a highly integrated system throughout our entire bodies. We are not the machines of reason and logic that we previously thought we were. As Richard Restak, author of several books about the brain, states, "We are not thinking machines, we are feeling machines that think."

We have learned that it is important to better understand our internal systems: how we work, how we respond to outside stimuli, how we learn, how we recall experiences, and, ultimately, what activates what parts of our internal systems when we interact with others.

It's useful to make a distinction between the brain and the mind. For simplicity, we will define the brain as "the organ of thought and neural coordination" and the mind as "the process that regulates the flow of energy and information throughout our bodies."

A quick overview of this new understanding of the mind includes four aspects of the brain that are relevant to understanding how people change:

1. The three-part structure
2. Right and left hemispheres
3. Neuroplasticity
4. Mirror neurons

"But I'm a Salesperson, Not a Brain Scientist"

We promise not to get too sciencey. What follows is just a quick primer, some fundamental concepts about the brain that we'll return to again and again in subsequent chapters. Once you grasp these basic concepts, you'll begin to understand how and why people decide to change, how the brain goes from "here's where I am today" to "here's something new I want to try." Possessing that knowledge will give you a major advantage as an influencer.

The Three-Part Structure

According to neuroscientist Paul D. MacLean, the brain developed in three stages (see Figure 2.1) over the course of human evolution, resulting in a "triune" structure (i.e., consisting of three parts). First came the reptilian (survival) brain, then the limbic (emotional) brain, then the neocortex (thinking) brain. Today, that's the same order in which our brains develop in the womb.

The *reptilian (survival) brain* is the most primitive brain structure, making up the part of the brain that originally

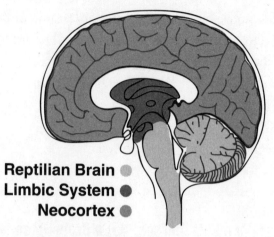

Reptilian Brain ●
Limbic System ●
Neocortex ●

Figure 2.1 The Evolution-Designed Brain

dominated the forebrains of reptiles and birds. Every species with a central nervous system has this structure. The survival brain regulates basic survival functions such as breathing and blood flow as well as instinctual behaviors related to aggression, dominance, territoriality, ritual displays, and the "fight or flight" decision in response to danger. When you instinctively swerve to miss an oncoming car in your lane, that's the highly evolved survival brain in action. You don't stop to think, you don't weigh the options, you don't consider pros and cons—you react.

Approximately two hundred million years ago, when the first mammals appeared, the *limbic (emotional) brain* evolved. Surrounding the survival brain like a doughnut, the limbic system gave mammals a unique capability—to *feel*. The emotional brain is what separates mammals from other species and gives them the ability to evaluate their conditions: "Is this good or bad?" As such, it's the primary part of the brain that motivates our actions (and even our reasoning and thought) and gives us the ability to learn, remember, adapt, and change. It's the limbic brain that draws us to what feels good and repels us from what doesn't. The limbic brain is believed to be responsible for motivation and emotion.

Like the limbic brain, the *neocortex (thinking) brain* is also found uniquely in mammals, but it is massively larger, proportionately, in humans than in other mammals. It's what makes humans distinctly different from all other species. The newest and least evolved part of the brain, the neocortex forms the outer layer and confers the ability for language, abstraction, planning, perception, and the capacity to recombine facts to form ideas. In short, the neocortex gives humans the unique advantage of advanced thought. But with this newest part of the brain comes a disadvantage, too: we can think too much.

The Brain's Operating System

Aristotle put forth the idea of "proportionality," proclaiming that our emotions are in equal and direct proportion to our reason. It was a compelling idea for its time, but just as technology eventually showed us that Earth is not the center of the universe, technology has also revealed that reason and emotion are not equals at the center of our internal universe. In fact, our emotions drive our reason.

As author and success coach Tony Robbins told the audience during his presentation at the 2006 TED conference, "I believe that the invisible force of internal drive, activated, is the most important thing in the world. . . . I believe *emotion* is the force of life."

Neuroscientists would concur. Thanks to new technologies, scientists have been able to map the brain's neural pathways, the specific routes by which information travels inside our heads. One important fact they've learned is that information flows from the inside out—from the survival brain, to the emotional brain, to the thinking brain. Since the emotional brain gets information before the thinking brain, it is capable of functioning independently of the neocortex, subconsciously, without cognitive thought. This makes sense, in evolutionary terms, because the emotional brain was there long before the thinking brain.

In his seminal book *Emotional Intelligence,* Daniel Goleman describes the limbic (emotional) system as the brain's first responder. All sensory information goes there first. The limbic system processes the information and sends its response to the thinking brain, which then produces its own response. The brain, therefore, produces an emotional response before it produces a cognitive one.

The limbic system is like the operating system on your computer. All of the rest of your "software"—your thinking brain—sits atop this operating system (figuratively and literally) and is dependent upon it. You might say that our emotions have a mind of their own. Our rationality relies on our emotions. We're hard-wired to feel first, think second.

In cases where sensory information carries little or no emotional weight, the thinking brain can assume a dominant role. But in cases where strong emotions are involved, the limbic system plays the main role in our behavior. The more intense an emotion, the more dominant the limbic system's response.

In the world of selling, the subject of emotional connection has always been considered off limits, too touchy-feely. No more. Now that we know emotion is what drives people to do what they do—what drives buyers to buy—it's a subject we can't afford not to focus on. Logic and reason, while still factors in a buyer's decision, are more likely to figure in after the fact, as a means of justifying a decision driven by emotion.

Like Dating a StairMaster

In the opening scene of *The Social Network*, Harvard student and future Facebook founder Mark Zuckerberg (played by Jesse Eisenberg) sits at a small table in a crowded bar with his girlfriend from Boston University, Erica (Rooney Mara). Zuckerberg is obsessed with getting into one of the exclusive Harvard final clubs. He gives Erica a highly detailed, highly logical explanation of why it's so important for him to do so. And then he logically asserts that she should be grateful to be his girlfriend. He tells her that if he gets in, he'll be taking her to events and gatherings, and she'll be meeting people she wouldn't normally meet.

"What is that supposed to mean?" she says.

"Wait. Settle down."

"What is it supposed to *mean*?" Erica says. "I'm going back to my dorm."

"Wait," says Zuckerberg. "Is this real?"

"Yes."

"Then I apologize."

But Erica has had enough of his logical, calculating, insulting behavior. She keeps telling him she's leaving to go study. He repeatedly tells her she doesn't have to study.

"Why do you keep saying I don't have to study?" she finally says, exasperated.

"Because you go to B.U.," Zuckerberg says. "Want to get some food?"

"It's exhausting," she says. "Going out with you is like dating a StairMaster. I think we should just be friends."

"I don't want friends," Zuckerberg says.

"I was just being polite," Erica says. "I have no intention of being friends with you." She takes a deep breath. "Look, you are probably going to be a very successful computer person. But you're going to go through life thinking that girls don't like you because you're a nerd. And I want you to know from the bottom of my heart that that won't be true. It'll be because you're an asshole."

Right Brain, Left Brain

Zuckerberg, as he's portrayed in the movie, functions on a purely intellectual level. He's clearly brilliant, but his mind seems disconnected from his heart. He wants a girlfriend, but he's incapable of establishing a real emotional connection with the girl sitting right across the table from him. He has all the right answers, but he can't open his mouth without saying something insensitive. He has zero social cognition, zero empathy, zero relationship skills. He comes off as rude and cold.

But whereas Erica sees Zuckerberg's behavior as a personal failing, a neuroscientist might see it as a matter of left brain versus right brain. (It's time for a little more science.) The neocortex—the thinking brain—is separated into two halves, or hemispheres. The brain architectures, types of cells, types of neurotransmitters, and receptor subtypes are all distributed between the two hemispheres in a markedly asymmetric fashion. As a result, the two hemispheres perform different functions and are responsible for processing different kinds of information. Think of the two halves as parallel but different processors; they give the human brain the ability to process information more effectively and exponentially faster.

The *left hemisphere* is primarily concerned with linear reasoning functions of language such as grammar and word production; numerical computation (exact calculation, numerical comparison, estimation); and direct fact retrieval. The left brain is analytical, logical, and rational. It thinks in literal terms and loves to solve problems and label things. It's the side of the brain that craves information. Give it some information, and it'll want more information about the information it just got.

The *right hemisphere,* on the other hand, is said to be the creative and emotional side of the human brain. It is primarily concerned with the holistic reasoning functions of language such as intonation and emphasis; approximate calculations and estimations; as well as pragmatic and contextual under-standing (i.e., "common sense").* The right brain thinks in pictures, images, and metaphors. It has the capacity to visual-ize and conceptualize. Social cognition resides in the right brain as well. All autobiographical memories are stored on the right. "Our right hemisphere gives us a more direct sense of the whole body, our waves and tides of emotions, and the pictures of lived experience that make up our autobiographi-cal memory," writes Daniel Seigel in *Mindsight.* "The right brain is the seat of our emotional and social selves." The right brain is also directly connected to the limbic system and to the central nervous system—to all of our senses. As Jill Bolte Tayler puts it in *My Stroke of Insight,* "We are all kinestheti-cally connected through our right sides."

The left brain says "no" because it becomes paralyzed from too little or too much information. The right brain says "yes"

---

* See Insup Taylor and M. Martin Taylor (1990), *Psycholinguistics: Learning and Using Language,* Englewood Cliffs, NJ: Prentice Hall, p. 367; S. Dehaene, E. Spelke, P. Pinel, R. Stanescu, and S. Tsivkin (1999), "Sources of Mathematical Thinking: Behavioral and Brain-Imaging Evidence," *Science* 284 (5416): 970–974, doj:10.1126/science.284. 5416.970, PMID 10320379; and Dehaene Stanislas, Piazza Manuela, Pinel Philippe, Cohen Laurent (2003), "Three Parietal Circuits for Number Processing," *Cognitive Neuropsychology* 20 (3): 487–506, doj:10.1080/02643290244000239, PMID 20957581.

because it can imagine the possibilities and use intuition to fill in gray areas. We make decisions primarily with our right brain. Think of the college you attended, the car you drive, the home you bought, the significant other you chose to spend your life with, the names of your children, the political party you favor. If these were all logical, left-brain decisions, all of us—or at least all of us in similar circumstances—would drive the same car, the one that gets us from point *a* to point *b* most affordably and efficiently. There would be *one* right car, the logical choice. We'd also belong to the same political party, live in the same neighborhood in the same kind of house, marry the same kinds of men or women, and have the same number of children with the same names. Because there would be one right answer.

Of course, we don't live our lives by logic. Every day, we make subjective decisions based on intuition, emotion, and the experiential memory that resides on an autobiographical shelf of the right brain.

But as salespeople, we've been taught to help buyers make a decision using logic. We've been taught to help them solve problems. It's little wonder that at some point in the buy cycle, buyers often get paralyzed and decide to maintain the status quo. Up until now, we haven't been speaking to their right brains. We haven't reached their emotional centers, the place where decisions are actually made. We've been selling like computers, not people. Can you imagine having Mark Zuckerberg sell to you?

What Kind of Brain Are You?

In our Story Leaders workshops, we train a lot of salespeople with engineering backgrounds, people whose job it is to sell to other engineers. And a lot of them tell us, "I'm a left-brainer."

Which is to say, their right brains are telling them they're left brainers.

That you have to be one or the other is a myth. Research shows that while one side is dominant at any point in time, both the left and right hemispheres operate simultaneously, all the time, in all of us. Sometimes, however, as a result of understimulation or underdevelopment, one side can become disproportionately dominant. Such is the case with the Mark Zuckerberg character in *The Social Network*. He's so left brain that he can barely connect with another human being. But the good news for the Zuckerbergs of the world is that they can change. Science has shown that, even in adults, the brain retains its plasticity.

Old Dogs *Can* Learn New Tricks

For a long time, everyone believed sales was a left-brain game. Today that view is being challenged more and more. In *A Whole New Mind: Why Right-Brainers Will Rule the Future*, Daniel Pink posits that the future of global business belongs not to the left-brainers but to people with highly developed right-brain skills.

But when we focus on right-brain skills in our workshops, senior sales executives are often skeptical. "You can't teach an old dog new tricks," they say. It's an objection based on the belief that we lose the ability to learn as we get older. Thankfully, it's also a myth.

Science has established that plasticity in the brain is a constant throughout our lives. "Plasticity" refers to the brain's ability to change and grow by making new synaptic connections to form new thoughts and ideas. Experience is what drives these changes in the brain. In the past 10 years or so, scientists have come to understand that we are constantly shaping our brain structure with every new experience. While it's true that this process occurs more rapidly in children, it nevertheless continues into adulthood.

It's this simple: we have new experiences; the brain makes new connections; new memories are formed. The brain constantly changes, grows, learns. Even in the old dogs among us.

One key factor in this process is the emotional weight of our experiences. Memories are formed in the limbic area, the emotional brain. The stronger the emotion associated with an experience, the better we remember it. If you're studying for a test, for instance, you're far more likely to remember the material if you have an emotional reaction to it, if you *feel* something. In the long run, we tend to remember more clearly the way an experience made us feel rather than the facts and details associated with that experience.

Monkey See, Monkey Do

Human beings, it turns out, are genetically wired to be empathetic.

When we see someone smile, we are inclined to smile ourselves. When we see someone suffering, we are inclined to feel their pain. And we all know what happens when we see someone yawn.

In the past 20 years, neuroscientists have discovered a physical basis for empathy. The brain is made up of tens of billions of cells called "neurons," a special cell that sends electrochemical signals to other neurons. Studies show that some of these neurons have mirroring behaviors. A "mirror neuron" is a neuron that fires both when an animal acts with intent and when the animal observes the same action being performed with intent by another. It essentially "mirrors" the behavior of the other, as though the observer itself were acting.

Intent is important because it arises from the brain's emotional center. If you pick up a glass of water because you're thirsty, you're likely to trigger mirror neurons in your dinner partner's brain. But if you act without intent—if you simply pick up the glass and put it down—you're unlikely to trigger mirror neurons. For the same reason, a fake yawn is much less likely to be mirrored than a real one. The degree of intent (i.e., emotion) is also important. The stronger the observed intent, the stronger the mirroring. Watching a waiter perform the Heimlich maneuver on a choking restaurant patron will produce a much stronger mirroring effect than watching your coworker perform the Heimlich on a dummy in a training session.

Mirror neurons were discovered by scientists studying macaque monkeys in the early 1990s. The scientists implanted devices in the monkeys' brains so they could observe neurons "lighting up." When JoJo the monkey watched another monkey eat a banana, for instance, the same neurons fired in JoJo's brain as when JoJo himself ate a banana. (Today, brain imaging devices allow scientists to make such observations noninvasively.)

Subsequently, mirror neurons have been discovered in humans as well. Their existence in humans essentially means that we have the power to be emotionally contagious. We can create a sense of well-being in others, just as we can create unhappiness or pain. As Mark Ghoulston writes in *Just Listen: Discover the Secret to Getting Through to Absolutely Anyone*, "We constantly mirror the world."

Later in the book, we'll discuss the important role that mirror neurons can play in sales, particularly with regard to storytelling and empathetic listening.

Solving a Problem Is Not the Answer

So ends our quick primer on recent developments in neuroscience.

Obviously, we've barely scratched the surface. For the purposes of this book, though, all you need to know are the three-part structure of the brain, the right and left hemispheres, plasticity, and mirror neurons. These are the key concepts that have reshaped our understanding of selling by demystifying how people decide to act and, by extension, how buyers decide to buy. All along we believed that the decision to buy was a linear, logical one when in fact it is primarily an emotional one, governed by the limbic system and the right brain. By knowing this, we have a greater insight into what great salespeople are doing. We know that attempting to "solve a buyer's problem" isn't the full story. In fact, it's only a small part of the story.

The new discoveries in the sciences have shifted our paradigm of selling. Decision making is not a problem-solving process, so neither should be the business of selling. In the pages that follow, we present a new model of selling based on a new understanding of how people really decide to change.

CHAPTER 3

The Hidden Power of Vulnerability

[Imperfections are not inadequacies; they are reminders that we're all in this together.

—Dr. Brené Brown]

Detective Anthony Terrell

Detective Anthony Terrell knew every second counted. Weaving through Los Angeles rush hour traffic, the 20-year veteran and LAPD lead hostage negotiator was en route to an ugly standoff. More than 30 officers, including the SWAT team, were already on the scene. Inside the house, Robert, an alcoholic in his fifties, was holding his wife and children at gunpoint. Things hadn't been going well for Robert. After he was fired from his job as a clerk at the DMV, his wife had kicked him out. Now he was planning to take his family's life and then his own.

The police tried to reason with Robert. They told him they had 15 squad cars blockading a three-block radius and all the firepower they needed to end the situation. Their rifles were trained on every window in the house. There was no escape.

"Either you come out," the captain said into his bullhorn, "or we come in."

"Shut up!" Robert screamed.

"At least let your family go," the captain said. "They have nothing to do with this."

"I'm not coming out," Robert said, "and neither are they."

By the time Detective Terrell arrived, the SWAT team was ready to storm the house. Terrell's job was to get Robert to release his family and surrender, but this would be difficult, because he had little time and Robert had little to live for: if Robert didn't give up, he was going to be shot and killed; if he gave up, he was likely going to prison.

The detective quickly established phone contact. With extensive training in psychology and more than 10 years experience negotiating in crisis situations, Terrell didn't bother trying to reason with Robert. Rather, the detective knew that his first order of business was to establish an emotional connection. He needed to put aside his personal feelings about Robert—a monster threatening to kill his own wife and kids—and convince Robert that he was on Robert's side, get him to think, "That guy is like me."

Once he had Robert on the line, Terrell introduced himself. "Robert," he said, "I can't imagine what you're going through. I've been in situations where I felt like there was no way out. I actually lost everything—my job, my home, my best friend—all at the same time. It might not be the situation you're in, but I remember how bad it was."

Terrell didn't try to convince Robert to give up. He didn't ask any questions. He just held his breath and waited.

Finally, Robert said, "When was that?"

And that's when Terrell knew he had an opening to connect with Robert. He told Robert a little about the darkest time in his life. Then he asked, "Do you want to tell me what's going on with you? It's okay if you don't, but I do want to know."

Robert eventually told Terrell he didn't feel like he could face his kids after losing his job and getting kicked out of the house. He was angry at his wife. He believed the easiest way out would be to end it for them all. Once Robert opened up, it was only minutes before Terrell was able to negotiate a surrender that saved the lives of Robert, his wife, and his kids.

Going First

As a student of psychology, Detective Terrell understood the power of "going first"—showing his own vulnerability as a way of getting Robert to open up and show his. By going first, Terrell essentially gave Robert permission to share his problems.

Outside of the corporate world, the power of vulnerability is well known. It's the basis for trust. The thinking goes: *If he's willing to open up and be vulnerable, then he must trust me, in which case it's safe for me to open up and share something in return.* When we allow ourselves to be seen—really seen—we create the potential for emotional connection. Research shows that self-disclosure is a common feature of healthy relationships.

Research also points to an instinctive response to vulnerability—the desire to reciprocate. Remember mirror neurons from Chapter 2? Mirror neurons are brain cells that fire both when we act and when we observe the same action performed with intent by another. They essentially "mirror" the behavior of the other, as though we ourselves were acting. Mirror neurons help explain why vulnerability is contagious. When people see us opening up and being authentic, they're inclined to open up and be authentic themselves. We are all imperfect—it's a universal truth. And, ironic as it seems, we trust people more when they're willing to expose themselves as imperfect. Allowing ourselves to be seen as vulnerable fosters an environment of openness and leads to trust.

In the business world, however, vulnerability is often mistaken for weakness. Salespeople have traditionally been trained to have all the answers, to be superhuman, to be perfect. But it's hard to connect with perfection. As buyers, our BS meters go off. We know nobody's perfect; we know nobody has all the answers. Also, when a seller presents herself as having all the answers, her attitude is contagious. A buyer is inclined to think: *Everything is good with her? Then everything is good with me, too.* As in: *There's nothing I need to buy.*

But in many cases, selling something to someone requires the buyer to more or less *admit* that change is necessary—to admit that everything *isn't* good. As in "I have a problem" or "my situation isn't ideal" or "I've made a mistake." This is particularly true when the sale involves something that is new to the buyer. In these cases, our success as sellers depends on buyers showing vulnerability by admitting imperfection. It's a lot easier for them to open up if we as sellers go first.

Ben's Story: Alana

I learned the danger of perfectionism first-hand from my therapist, Alana. As salespeople, we're taught that we should be flawless: we should possess complete knowledge of our products. We should have complete knowledge of the sales situation. We should have all the answers to our customers' questions. We should be able to overcome all of our customers' objections. I was as guilty of this attitude as anyone, if not more so. I'd bought into it for my whole career, as both a salesperson and a trainer of salespeople.

A couple of years ago, I went in for a session with my therapist, Alana, prior to an important workshop with the senior executives of a new client. I felt I had to pull off a perfect workshop in order to sell the company more workshops. I would need to be at the top of my game and look the part too, right down to my best suit and a nice, clean haircut. I told Alana I was feeling a lot of anxiety about the workshop.

"I can't blow it," I said. "I have to be absolutely perfect."

Alana's reaction surprised me. It was practically a reprimand.

"Who do you think you have to be, Ben?" she said. "You just don't get it, do you?"

And then she proceeded to tell me a story. She said that in the psychology profession, after graduation, you have to put in a number of hours as an intern before you're fully licensed to practice on your own. She did her hours at a battered women's shelter in south-central Los Angeles. She led a weekly evening group therapy session with several young women, mostly teenaged moms, some of them homeless. One by one, she said, the women in the group began to open up—all of them, that is, except for one. During the sixth week, this particular young woman came up to Alana after the session and said she wasn't coming back. Alana asked why. The young woman regarded Alana as if the answer were self-evident.

"Look at you," she said, "with your Gucci bag, your expensive shoes, your perfect hair, your perfect smile. Why would *I* ever open up to *you?*"

Alana was devastated. For six weeks, she'd been trying to connect with this woman. At 30, fresh out of graduate school, Alana thought she'd been doing all the right things. She thought it was her job to look the part of a successful professional and to be an expert in her field. But in the process of trying to project an image of perfection, she'd managed to scare off one of the people she was supposed to help.

"When you talked about needing to be perfect in your workshop," Alana told me during our session, "you reminded me of myself, of how I was back then."

I immediately identified with Alana's story. What she said next made a lot of sense to me. She explained that the best teachers teach by sharing their mistakes and what they've learned. She used the analogy of ex-addict counselors who help recovering drug addicts.

"We don't connect with perfection," she said. "We connect with people who've been there."

That day's session with Alana was more than just a reality check; it was a revelation. Alana gave me the confidence to be imperfect. She also helped me understand that not only is imperfection natural and human, it's absolutely necessary if we hope to connect to other people.

Shame and Courage

Dr. Brené Brown, a research professor at the University of Houston Graduate College of Social Work, has spent

Shame ⟵⟶ Courage

Figure 3.1 The Spectrum of Shame and Courage
Source: Dr. Brené Brown

the past 10 years studying vulnerability, fear, authenticity, shame, and courage. Her research led her to conceive a spectrum on which shame and courage occupy opposite ends (see Figure 3.1).

Research shows that the only people who don't experience shame have no capacity for human connection or empathy—people with psychopathic disorders. Shame is universal among the rest of us. "Shame is the most primitive human affect or emotion that we experience," says Brown. "Everyone has it. Nobody wants to talk about it. Yet the less we talk about it, the more we have it."

Shame and fear are the emotions that prevent us from being vulnerable—the fear of not being successful enough, not rich enough, not smart enough. According to Brown, it drives two primary "tapes" in our minds: "never good enough" and "who do you think you are?" The more shame we have surrounding a given issue, the less we talk about it.

Shame is best understood, says Brown, as "the fear of disconnection." Shame feels the same for men and women, but the cultural drivers of shame—the messages and expectations that fuel it—are very much gender based. For women, shame is about not being perfect, not being everything to everyone, not being thin enough, not being able to do it all and smile the whole time. For men, the primary cultural "rule" that drives shame is "do not be perceived as weak." Men are expected to be emotionally stoic. In the world of sales, however, we believe the fear of perceived weakness drives both men *and* women, to the extent that all salespeople are expected to be superhuman.

When we ask students in the workshop, "How many of you struggle with shame?" no hands go up. It's a silent epidemic. But if we ask, "How many of you struggle with perfectionism?" we get a lot of responses. Brown sees shame and perfectionism as inextricably linked. "Shame," she says, "is the birthplace of perfectionism. Where we struggle with perfectionism, we struggle with shame."

"The hard thing," she says, "is you can't get rid of shame. So what can we do? We can be resilient." In other words, tame it. Her research shows that people with high shame resilience have several things in common: They understand shame and what triggers it. They talk about it. They have more authenticity. They live with a stronger sense of love and belonging. And they tell their stories.

The key to resilience is courage, which comes from the Latin *cor*, meaning "heart." We must have the heart to be imperfect. "To me," says Brown, "courage is the ability to tell your story and like who you are in the process of doing that. And that's hard."

You *Can* Go There

During our Story Leaders workshops, we delve into vulnerability on the second day. Sometimes it's a tough sell—pun intended. Once, a young woman in her early thirties—a well-dressed, highly educated saleswoman—stood up and objected.

"There's no way we can go there in a business conversation," she said. "It's too touchy-feely. We would look weak in front of a buyer."

That stirred up a hornet's nest in the workshop. Half of the students were on her side, the other half on ours.

Believe me, we understand why vulnerability can be so hard for salespeople. We're salespeople ourselves; we've experienced the fear of having a buyer think poorly of us; we've been there. And we realize that the idea of showing vulnerability can seem counterintuitive. By revealing ourselves, we worry we will appear weak or submissive. Like most salespeople today, we were taught that in order to be "consultative, trusted advisors," we must be perceived as experts who have all the answers.

The truth of the matter is, we agree. A salesperson absolutely *should* be an expert in his or her field. We just disagree that trying to come off as an expert—presenting yourself as superhuman—is an effective way to sell. Research and other disciplines have proven that the opposite is true. We don't lose power by showing our vulnerability; we *gain* power.

But there's another problem. Many of us simply don't know *how* to be vulnerable. We lack the vocabulary of vulnerability. Showing vulnerability involves the use of recall and self-reflection, putting language (left-brain processing) around emotions and autobiographical memories (right-brain processing).

If you're convinced of the value of vulnerability but aren't sure how to go about showing it in a business setting, don't worry. In subsequent chapters, we'll take you through the process, step by step, of developing the necessary language and narrative skills.

> **Exercise**
>
> Write down three mistakes you have made, three mistakes your company has made, and three mistakes your clients have made. Be willing to share these three mistakes with your family and friends. Now, think of a mistake that you could never tell a friend or colleague, something you wouldn't reveal. Why? What if your friend shared the same mistake with you?

What Therapists Do

When it comes to understanding the power of vulnerability, the sales industry is still primitive. Therapy is but one of many fields that has long understood vulnerability better than we have. Like salespeople, therapists need their clients to open up to them. But unlike salespeople, therapists aren't trained to interrogate their clients with questions. Instead, they use a range of techniques based on a fuller understanding of trust and emotional connection. (Too Much Information alert: If the following sections are too technical for you, feel free to skip ahead to Mike's story about Juliet.)

Inclusion and Presence
One of these techniques involves inclusion and presence. *Inclusion* means putting oneself into the experience of the patient as much as possible, feeling it as if in one's own body. When a therapist does this, it confirms the patient's existence. By imagining the experience of the client, in a sense, the therapist makes the experience real. By making contact

with the patient in this way and not aiming to "move" the patient—by meeting the patient and not aiming to make the patient different—the therapist supports the patient in growing by identification with his or her own experience. Dialogue between therapist and client requires not only practicing inclusion but also a certain kind of *presence*: authenticity, transparency, and humility. Both therapist and patient must connect with their whole selves, including their flaws. Inclusion and presence require self-disclosure on the part of the therapist. In this model, think of the client as the final authority. If the patient says, "You don't understand," the therapist doesn't understand.

Commitment and Surrender to the Between

An indispensable core aspect of therapy is the commitment to dialogue, the surrender to what emerges between the participants in the dialogue when the therapist and the patient contact each other—without the therapist aiming for a particular response. Conditions for maximum growth and healing are created when the therapist practices inclusion with authentic presence and commits to what emerges in the contact. This requires that the therapist not be committed to any predetermined outcome.

In this approach, the therapist also changes. The therapist is touched, feels pain, gets satisfaction from contact with the patient, and learns from the contact. By accepting that the patient's perception of the therapist might accurately point to a blind spot in the therapist's self-awareness, the therapist also grows. This is especially true when the patient criticizes the therapist. For the patient, this can be an experience in which her opinions and feelings are respected and in which she is able to recognize the therapist (in whom she has invested time, money, and respect) as an ordinary human being.

Mike's Story: Juliet

Perhaps because I'm known as a "sales and messaging" guy, a number of friends and acquaintances have asked me for advice regarding things in their personal lives. Not long ago, my dear friend Juliet asked me for help with her profile on Match.com, the online dating website.

Juliet is in her mid-forties, very fit, very vital, and very attractive. She gets *lots* of inquiries on Match.com. Juliet is also a recent cancer survivor. She beat a very aggressive, fast-growing cancer. When she was ready to start dating again, she was unsure whether to share her battle against cancer in her Match.com profile.

Most of her friends advised her not to mention that she's a cancer survivor. But the way I saw it, it's obviously a very big deal, and it would have to come out sooner or later. I suggested that if she put "cancer survivor" in her profile and got just one response a month, at least she'd have the peace of mind of knowing that her date already knew, and she wouldn't have to dread bringing up the subject.

So Juliet did it. She changed her profile to indicate she'd had cancer. And very quickly, her "winks" and matches *doubled.*

At first, I was surprised, but I shouldn't have been. Juliet's experience validated everything I've come to understand about vulnerability. I ended up putting her story on our Story Leaders blog. Within a day, we had more comments than for any previous blog posting. Everyone wanted to share their experiences with vulnerability.

Mike's Story: Bob Populorum

During my years at Xerox Computer Services, one of my mentors was a salesman named Bob Populorum. Bob was 10 or 11 years older than I was. He'd been smart enough to get into Northwestern, and while he was there, he'd taken an interest in human psychology. By the time I knew him, he was a keen student of human nature.

As a parent, Bob often found himself at social events—PTA meetings, school fund-raisers, and so forth—with other parents. When the small talk inevitably turned to kids, the parents inevitably turned to bragging. You know, the "who has a better kid" contest. If the first dad mentioned that his oldest daughter was an aspiring concert pianist, the next dad might mention that *his* daughter had gotten into Yale, and then the next dad might start in about *his* daughter's Olympic chances, and so on.

Bob never cared for this sort of one-upmanship. He was much more interested in having real, authentic conversations. He understood that if you lead with a story about how great your kid is, chances are that's what you'll get in return. And so he began to experiment at these gatherings. Instead of starting with a boast about his kids, he'd start with a little humor.

"I have five kids," he'd say, keeping a straight face. "One of each."

Then he'd shoot from the heart. "The first four are all doing great—good grades, well rounded, volunteer work, you name it. But oh, that number five." Bob would proceed to talk about his youngest son's problems: flunking out of school, shoplifting, drug rehab, the whole nine yards.

Whenever Bob did this, without fail, the other parents would then open up and share stories about their difficulties with their kids. Suddenly, Bob and the other parents weren't engaged in a "top this" contest; they were forming real emotional connections. By having the courage to be vulnerable first, Bob was encouraging other parents to be vulnerable, too.

Bob is the person who helped me understand the importance of vulnerability in gaining a stranger's trust. And it's as true in sales as it is at PTA meetings. A stranger is more likely to buy from you if he trusts you, becomes curious about what you have to offer, believes you have his best interests at heart.

Bob used to say that there is a "veneer of bullshit" between any two strangers, and as we all know, that's especially true with a seller and buyer.

"Until you break through that veneer of bullshit," he'd tell me, "you have no chance of selling anything."

Vulnerability in Sales

It takes courage to admit your flaws first. It's a risk. But it's a risk with enormous potential rewards. When a buyer meets with a salesperson, the buyer expects to feel "sold to." The buyer's reaction, based on her previous experiences with salespeople, is likely to be some variation of fight, flight, or freeze. But you can overcome a buyer's expectations and preconceived notions and give her a chance to be truly receptive to you by taking a chance and being vulnerable first.

Granted, being vulnerable is more easily said than done. Most salespeople we know have been indoctrinated with a left-brain approach. We've been trained with hundreds of PowerPoint slides that cover every salient detail regarding our markets, our products, our pricing, company procedures and systems, contract approval processes, and so on. Make no mistake—a salesperson needs to know all of this and more. But these things aren't enough if you want to forge emotional connections with buyers.

So how do you teach people who have been trained to turn off their feelings to be vulnerable? It's a question we've confronted in our Story Leaders workshops, which are a work in progress that we're constantly fine-tuning.

At a recent workshop, we felt we made a giant leap forward in teaching highly disciplined left-brain thinkers (in this case, a group of engineers and scientists) to take the risk of being vulnerable by using the whole brain rather than just the left brain. In order to do so, they had to (1) have the courage to overcome the survival instincts of the left brain, (2) put narrative around feelings they had never articulated or shared with anyone, and, (3) most importantly, open themselves to the experience of feeling the connected space between two human beings.

Our workshops last two and a half days. On the first day of this particular workshop, we asked the participants to build a "Who I Am" story (see Chapter 6)—a step we normally take later in the workshop, as this is usually the hardest story to build. Basically, it's the story of how you, as a person in the world, ended up across the desk from this person (the buyer), in this moment in time, representing this company and this product. The story requires that the teller take a risk and show vulnerability.

The next day, we began to teach "story tending." Story tending is covered in detail later on, too, in Chapter 7. For now, all you need to know is that we conduct small-group exercises in which one person is a storyteller, one is a story tender, and one is an observer.

In this particular workshop, the teller in each group was instructed to tell his or her Who I Am story—created on the previous day—to the story tender (the listener). The tellers were asked to tell their stories at a slower-than-normal pace, allowing the listener to "tend" the story with sincere curiosity and a lot of encouragement, with comments such as, "It sounds like that was a real struggle for you. Can you tell me more?"

What surprised us was how emotional the storytellers became when their personal stories were so sincerely tended. A couple of them actually wept. Through this exercise, our highly disciplined left-brain participants were able to experience the emotional connection that occurs when we truly feel heard, when our stories are closely listened to. The strong feelings they experienced were, in turn, proof positive of the power of taking a risk and showing vulnerability first.

Others Knew Better

The power of vulnerability is largely unknown in American business, but it's no secret in other fields. Dr. Brené Brown and other researchers have devoted their careers to further understanding its power. Still others have been putting its power to use in both professional and personal settings. Detective Terrell opened up to a potential murderer—and in the process saved both the man and his family. Ben's therapist, Alana, learned the hard way the dangers of trying to project an air of perfection, of refusing to be vulnerable. Juliet openly shared the most difficult aspect of her life—and was rewarded with an outpouring of support and human connection. Bob Populorum, in confessing his youngest son's struggles, was able to establish trust and authenticity

46

in a setting that otherwise encouraged shallow bragging. All of these people understood, at least intuitively, the power of vulnerability. And the best salespeople among us know it too. Remember John Scanlon in Chapter 1? Now it's time for the rest of the sales world to take notice.

We understand that you think this might be off limits, that this isn't what a salesperson should be doing, that showing vulnerability is a weakness, that it's too touchy-feely. We get it. But it's *not* touchy-feely. Vulnerability is a key ingredient—perhaps *the* key ingredient—to emotional buy-in, to cutting through the "veneer of bullshit." It's what other disciplines do, and it's what works in sales, too.

Exercise

This basic exercise will help you understand the power of connection that comes with taking a risk and being vulnerable.

Share something you're not proud of with someone you care about. Start with a loved one—your child, your partner, your best friend, a sibling, or a parent. Reveal your vulnerability slowly. When the other person gives you an opportunity to be sincerely curious about their reaction to your story, let yourself fully experience the emotional connection.

CHAPTER 4

Our Brains on Story

> We make sense of the events of our lives through stories.
> —Daniel J. Siegel, M.D., author of *Mindsight*

The Barriers

We tend to put up barriers to people trying to influence us, and for good reason. It's a natural defense mechanism. We do it to protect ourselves.

At the start of our Story Leaders workshops, we ask participants—usually a group of salespeople—to name the professions they trust the least. "Politicians!" is almost always the first answer, usually followed by "Salespeople!" And then, like clockwork, everyone in the room starts to laugh.

As salespeople, we know how difficult it is to build trust. Most of us have had bad experiences with salespeople ourselves. We know the uncomfortable feeling of being "sold to," the feeling of someone trying to use us for their own financial gain.

Once the laughter dies down, we ask, "Why?" Why do people have negative stereotypes about salespeople and politicians? We hear the same answers again and again: "Because they're manipulative." "Because they're in it only for themselves." "Because they try to get me to do what they want me to do." "Because they're slimy and dishonest."

Then we ask participants how they arrived at these perceptions. The obvious answer is past experience: all of the politicians we've seen embroiled in scandal, double-talking, reneging on campaign promises; all of the salespeople who've ever tried to sell us.

It's a harsh reality for those of us in sales. Getting people to believe in us is difficult enough. Getting people to change when they're predisposed to distrust us is even harder.

Reactive or Receptive?

Imagine walking into an electronics store to buy a DVD player. You've done a little homework and you more or less know what you want. Within 10 seconds, before you even find your aisle, a salesperson approaches and asks, "Can I help you, ma'am?"

Your automatic reply? "No, thanks, I'm just looking."

It's the kind of answer we give even when we're not just looking, even when we could use a little help. It's a natural defense against someone trying to influence us.

The reason for this automatic reply is revealed in the science of the mind. When our limbic area senses a threat, it sends a message to the reactive brain: "What do I need to do to be safe?" When the threat is great enough, we either go to fight or flight. At that point, our most primitive brain, the survival brain, kicks in and takes control.

For lesser threats, the message is processed by the side of the neocortex that reacts to danger: the left brain. The left brain can analyze the threat and determine how to deal with it. When we as sellers approach buyers, we are, by definition, activating the reactive side of their brains. When we lead with messages that make people feel like they're being "sold to" or that simply threaten their paradigms or dogmas, the reactive mind instinctually kicks into gear.

Think of the last time you had a heated political debate with someone. Can you recall the unpleasant visceral reaction of having your deeply held beliefs challenged? And it's not just contrary ideas that trigger your left brain. New ideas in general are met with resistance because we perceive them as trying to influence us to change.

But what if sellers could activate the right side of the brain, the receptive side?

The right side of the neocortex is responsible for the kinds of responses we want to trigger in others: "This feels good." "I am safe." "I am open to this." "I want to hear more." "This person [or idea] is not a threat to me."

Mike's Story: Sales Associate

I spent my first three years at Xerox Computer Services working in customer support. When my manager asked me to go into sales, I said no. He finally convinced me to do so, but only under one condition: I could keep my help-desk base salary, and if after six months I wanted to go back to the help desk, he would save a spot for me. I was given new business cards that said "sales associate." Right away, buyers started reacting differently to me. They seemed wary. It dawned on me that my new title was part of the problem. After a couple of weeks, I went back to my old business cards, the ones that said "customer support." Sure enough, buyers started treating me like they used to. I was back to being someone who was there to help them, not sell them.

Ben's Story: A Good Story Is the Antidote

Not long ago, I was in New York leading a Story Leaders workshop for Oracle. After one of the sessions, a salesperson and workshop student, Nic, invited me to the second annual Oracle Financial Services Forum, an event geared toward Wall Street CIOs. Oracle's president, Mark Hurd, was giving a breakfast keynote speech on the future of IT in financial services, particularly mobile technologies. About 80 executives were seated at tables on the main floor of the auditorium. More people filled the balcony, including many vendors and Oracle employees who wanted to hear what their president had to say.

All eyes turned to Mark when he arrived. After a few greetings, he strode to the podium, took his place behind the lectern, directed his assistant to load his PowerPoint presentation, and began discussing slides—slide after slide after slide.

After just a few minutes of Mark talking about Oracle's position in the marketplace, Oracle's mobility offerings, and so forth, Nic asked me to look across the room. I realized that almost no one was looking at Mark. The CIOs had their BlackBerrys and iPhones out, checking e-mail, eating breakfast, and so on. Nic and I were amazed. Here was Mark, the president of one of the world's largest companies, a man with a commanding presence, and hardly anyone in the room was giving him their full attention. It was almost as if Mark weren't even there.

Just then, Mark looked up from his slides and said, "A couple of weeks ago, I was in the car with my daughter, driving to the San Francisco airport, trying to check the status of my flight on my cell phone. I couldn't find it, and I was running out of patience. So my daughter says, 'Just relax, Dad.' Then she got out her iPhone and had the information I needed in about 30 seconds."

The story was short, personal, and to the point. Mark was saying that mobile devices are the future of communication because they've already been embraced by younger generations. But it wasn't the point of his story that got me so much as the *effect* of it. The moment he began, everyone in the room, without exception, turned their attention to Mark. The CIOs set aside their BlackBerrys, put down their knives and forks, and listened. And even when Mark returned to his slides, the audience stayed engaged, right through to the end of his presentation. People asked questions and took notes, and one of the CIOs even told a similar story about *his* teenaged daughter.

Once Upon a Time

What happened during Mark Hurd's speech was no surprise. Our minds are wired to respond to a story. It's intrinsic to who we are and how our brains function. As humans, we are natural story learners, storytellers, and story listeners.

Ever notice how the words *once upon a time* can calm a child? At bedtime, they're like magic. The child instantly relaxes. And the next night, without fail, the child asks, "Can you tell me another story?"

Stories have a similarly soothing effect on adults. When we hear "once upon a time" or "Can I tell you a story?" we nonconsciously tell ourselves, "Oh, it's just a story. I don't have to *do* anything or *decide* anything. I can just listen and enjoy." But at the same time we relax, we also focus and pay attention, because we are story learners, biologically wired to survive by learning through narrative. Our nonconscious mind is saying, "It's just a story," but it's also saying, "I'd better pay attention, I might learn something." This is the power of a story.

Facts, figures, lists, and statistics require us to do heavy mental lifting—left-brain work. Give the left brain some information, and it will immediately want details. Give the left brain those details, and it will immediately want more information. The left brain is constantly fighting to find answers. It has a low tolerance for gray areas. But give the left brain *too* much information—say, too many slides—and you might lose a listener's interest altogether.

By contrast, the right brain sees the big picture; it thinks in images, pictures, and stories. For this reason, story is an antidote to the critical left brain, offering a pathway around the barriers that we put up against people trying to influence us. Stories activate our limbic brain—our emotional center—because they contain the language of emotion. They also activate our sensory perception system, where all of our senses are kinesthetically connected. We experience a story in sensory terms in our imagination—we see it, we hear it, we smell it, we taste it, and we feel it.

We know from brain research that stories activate the right brain, but we also know it from experience. Simply put, stories *feel good*. On a visceral level, we are inclined to feel engaged with someone the moment that person says, "Hey, that reminds me of something that happened yesterday . . . "

Deciding to change isn't simply about logic, however much we'd like to believe so. It would be more accurate to say that we make decisions based on feelings, and then we use logic after the fact to justify our decisions. In relaxing the left brain and opening up the emotional right brain, stories cater to the part of the brain that decides to trust, to act—the part that says, "I'm going to change."

Can you imagine a better frame of mind to cultivate in a buyer? Making the decision to listen to someone, to change, or to buy is ultimately a right-brain activity. Stories just feel good to people. Since Mike and I started asking our customers, "Can I tell you a story?" neither of us has been turned down yet.

95,000 Years of Storytelling

Back when we first started teaching Story Leaders, we were talking about the power of story with Derek, an anthropologist friend of ours. Derek told us about a recent family vacation to Australia. While he was there, everyone, including his tour guide, kept telling him, "You have to take your family to Ayers Rock." Ayers Rock, known as Uluru to the aboriginal people, is a massive sandstone formation. Australia's most famous natural landmark, it is a sacred site to the Aborigines. Derek wanted to go, but Uluru is in the middle of a vast desert in the center of the continent, and it was midsummer, a blazing 105 degrees. The desert hardly seemed like a good destination for a family with young kids.

The anthropologist in Derek couldn't resist, though. After driving across the desert for several hours, he and his family were rewarded with a stunning sight, an island of sandstone rising more than 1,100 feet from the barren desert floor, with a circumference of almost six miles. But the exterior of Uluru wasn't what amazed them most. Inside the mountain are rooms. Aboriginal settlers used the rock as their home base more than 10,000 years ago. On the walls of these rooms are paintings that tell stories of danger, survival, medicine, the seasons, hunting, spices, and so on. In essence, these were *classrooms*, where aboriginal culture was passed down through the generations by way of visual stories—stories that are still there one hundred centuries later.

Derek told us that stories have been the primary means of conveying ideas since humans developed language some 95,000 years ago. They appear not only at Uluru but in the remnants of all ancient civilizations, including the Egyptian pyramids and Mayan ruins. As long as we've been communicating with each other, we've been telling stories, one way or another. As a species, we evolved as storytellers.

Brad Kerr's Story: A Family Tradition

I attended a Story Leaders workshop in August 2010. As the sales director of a large IT company, I was eager to improve my own sales effectiveness. At the same time, I was pretty skeptical. I got what Mike and Ben were saying about vulnerability and empathy and all that, but I didn't think it would fly at my company. It took my three-year-old son and five-year-old daughter to change my mind.

My first night home after the workshop, I sat down to dinner with my family and started asking my kids the usual questions: "What did you do today?" "Who did you play with?" "Did you have fun at school?" My son, Jack, was already too busy with his meatloaf to answer, and my daughter, Natalie, gave me the usual one-word replies: "Play." "Lauren." "Yes." Then we proceeded to eat in silence. It wasn't the first time I'd been disappointed that my kids wouldn't open up more. But this time, listening to the scrape of their forks, I thought back to the workshop and realized what the problem was: questions! I was doing no better with my kids than a salesman who interrogates his customers.

So I tried something new. I said, "Anybody want to hear a story?"

Immediately, Jack and Natalie looked up from their dinner. "Yes."

So I told them about my week in San Diego—meeting new people, going to dinner with my boss. It wasn't the most exciting story, but I remembered what I'd learned in the workshop and showed some vulnerability. "Daddy wasn't the best golf player," I said. And then I passed the torch. "So Natalie, what's been going on with you?"

Without missing a beat, she started telling me about school, how they were farming ants and how she and Lauren had played princesses on the playground while the boys were playing policeman. I couldn't believe how forthcoming she was. Then Jack jumped in with a story too. My wife shot me a look of disbelief. All I could do was smile.

Storytelling at dinner is a family tradition now. As soon as we sit down, one of the kids will say, "Raise your hand if you have a story." And we all raise our hands. Jack prides himself on telling the longest stories and will warn us beforehand: "This is going to be a long one!" Natalie loves to hear stories about Mommy and Daddy when we were kids. And my wife and I love hearing and telling stories, too. As I write this, I'm thinking about dinner tonight, when I'll tell them the story of how their story will be shared in a book forever.

Ben's Story: Zoe's History Lesson, Part Two

Remember the story of Zoe and her disdain for history, which I told in the Introduction? I'm happy to report that the problem didn't last. The next semester, Zoe's class studied Greek mythology, and this time the teacher didn't use a PowerPoint presentation on the Smart Board. Instead, she broke the class into groups and gave them a two-month assignment to study one of the myths and then perform it as a play for the rest of the class. The play was the final exam. Zoe got an A. Given the chance to learn through a story, she turned the corner in history class.

Story Learners

Dr. Jerome Bruner, one of the fathers of cognitive psychology, studied the profound effects of story on children. He observed that as early as the age of two, we are thinking and communicating in story. His research showed that babies organize their ideas in story, everything from "not more" to "I want." In the 1980s, his hypothesis led to a larger study that monitored and recorded the pre-language sounds of babies alone in their cribs. A group of linguists and psychologists at Harvard concluded that the sounds constituted attempts at storytelling. The findings ended up in a book, *Narratives from the Crib*.

In other words, even before we learn language, we use narrative to organize our thoughts and ideas. We think in story. We learn through story. By the time we're in school, most of us have heard thousands of them—fables, fairy tales, myths, lessons passed down to us from our parents, and so on. And because we're story learners, they tend to stick with us.

Ben's Story: The Boy Who Cried Wolf

A couple of years ago, I was in the backyard with my youngest daughter, Abby, when my wife came out and asked if I could help her do some work in the house.

"I'd be happy to," I said, "but I can't. My shoulder hurts."

Abby had the presence of mind to wait until my wife was back inside before she turned to me with a disapproving look. "Dad," she said, "remember the boy who cried wolf?"

Abby was six years old. It had probably been a year since I'd told her about the boy who cried wolf, but the story—and its lesson—had stuck with her. All I could do was put a finger to my lips and say, "Ssshhh."

Stages of the Storytelling Process

In George W. Bush's memoir, *Decision Points*, the ex-president relates a story about meeting with former Russian president Vladimir Putin. Early in the meeting, Putin was stiff and formal, mainly reading from prepared note cards. Exasperated, President Bush interrupted with a question: "Is it true your mother gave you a cross that you had blessed in Jerusalem?" The question prompted Putin to tell the story of how he almost lost the cross in a house fire, but firemen were able to retrieve it. "I felt the tension drain from the meeting room," writes Bush, recounting the moment. He then goes on to detail how he and Putin drew closer as Putin was telling the story and how, afterward, they remained more connected. ("I was able to get a sense of his soul," Bush famously said later. Given their subsequent difficulties, whether Putin "sold" Bush using story remains open to speculation.)

University of North Carolina professor Brian Sturm, who teaches storytelling and folklore, explains that the storytelling process works in seven distinct stages. His model reveals the effects of story on both the listener and teller.

Stage 1

The teller (T) and the listener (L) are engaged in conversation, an "active mode of consciousness." They are separate and may even be in opposition to or in competition with each other (see Figure 4.1).

Figure 4.1 Storytelling Process, Stage 1

Stage 2

The teller initiates a story (S) with some variation of "once upon a time" or "Can I tell you a story?" The story, as it begins, becomes a third entity in the relationship between the teller and listener (see Figure 4.2).

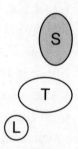

Figure 4.2 Storytelling Process, Stage 2

Stage 3

The teller becomes involved. As the story proceeds, the teller gets caught up in the story, reliving or at least reflecting on what is happening in it. At this stage, the listener begins to feel more connected with the teller, because the teller is no longer in opposition or competition but is instead involved in the story (see Figure 4.3).

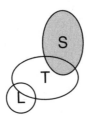

Figure 4.3 Storytelling Process, Stage 3

Stage 4

The listener becomes involved in the story. As the story proceeds, the listener begins to relive or reflect on what is happening in the story. The listener and teller begin to share the experience (see Figure 4.4).

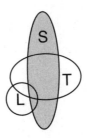

Figure 4.4 Storytelling Process, Stage 4

Stage 5

As the story becomes more compelling, the listener and teller become part of the story and therefore more closely connected. Note that both the teller and listener are "inside" the story; the story is bigger than either of them. The story is now the communicating entity, more so than the teller. The teller and listener are equals inside the story experience. Both are in the "story realm," a passive mode of consciousness or even an altered state of consciousness (see Figure 4.5).

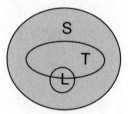

Figure 4.5 Storytelling Process, Stage 5

Stage 6

The teller begins to wrap up the story and withdraw from the story realm (see Figure 4.6).

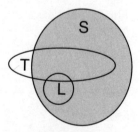

Figure 4.6 Storytelling Process, Stage 6

Stage 7

All stories have to end. The story is over but still remembered, leaving the listener and teller still connected, in a way that they weren't connected before the story began (see Figure 4.7).

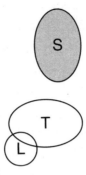

Figure 4.7 Storytelling Process, Stage 7

Needless to say, this process plays itself out with greater or lesser effectiveness depending upon the storytelling skills of the teller, the listening skills of the listener, and the quality of the story itself. However, it is not at all uncommon for people to be greatly moved or greatly influenced by stories that they hear from strangers. A perfect example of this (in written form) is the bestselling Chicken Soup series of books, which contain collections of personal stories.

CHAPTER 5

Story Building

> A story is the expression of how and why life changes. A story begins with balance, then something throws life out of balance, then a story goes on to describe how balance is restored.
> —Robert McKee

What Is Story?

As humans, we think and learn in terms of story. Story is intrinsic to being human.

The act of recounting stories involves drawing upon memories, which are stored in our right brain. Our right brain also gives us both social and emotional context for those memories. Building language around our memories and creating logical explanations, on the other hand, is the left brain's job; thus, storytelling is a whole-brain process. There's the *mental* detective work of piecing together the structure of a story and the *emotional* detective work of figuring out how we feel about it, how we convey those feelings, and what points we are making. As Dr. Daniel Siegel puts it, "When the left-mode drive to explain and the right-mode nonverbal and autobiographical processing are freely integrated, a coherent narrative emerges."

Change Is at the Heart of Story

If story is the expression of change in life, then an understanding of how change occurs will help us build our stories. Researchers who study change have made an interesting discovery about how passengers on sinking ships behave. Common sense suggests that passengers would jump into lifeboats as soon as they learn their ship is sinking. But that's not the case. In fact, most passengers do the opposite: they remain on board until the last possible moment. The reason? Fear of the unknown. Passengers are able to rationalize not getting into the lifeboats by kidding themselves, by inventing scenarios in which the ship might stop sinking. Their line of thinking is: "This ship is still above water. I don't know anything about that lifeboat. I'm not jumping until I have to."

Fear of the unknown is what prevents us from changing. Think of times in your life that you haven't changed even though you knew you should have, times you maintained the status quo out of fear of the unknown.

Change is slow. We resist it. It's part of human nature. Most of us change only when we feel we have to. We attempt to rationalize the status quo ("This ship is still above water") until we are forced to acknowledge that the status quo is untenable ("My feet are getting wet!").

The arc of change (Figure 5.1) presents a model of how things in life change. The line represents the intensity, over

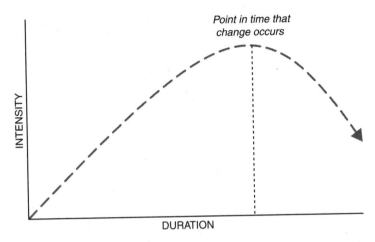

Figure 5.1 The Arc of Change

time, of the pressures that influence a given change. The peak of the line represents the point of change. Note that the change occurs only after a lot of pressure has built up over a lot of time.

Not coincidentally, models of story structure express a similar arc. In fact, experienced storytellers will tell you that story and change are inextricably linked. Viewed in this light, the study of story is also the study of how and why humans change, which is very relevant to sales. On the most basic level, selling requires people—our customers— to change, to overcome the fear of the unknown. As salespeople, then, it's important that we understand how change occurs in order to influence others.

In this chapter, we're going to give you a framework for recounting and building your stories step by step. It might not feel natural, especially at first. But the more stories you build, the more you'll begin to use this framework to think of your experiences in "storiable" terms.

Ben's Story: How Could I Ever Be a Storyteller?

One evening, Mike and I were sitting around at his house talking about the very best storytellers we knew.

"My grandmother," Mike said without hesitation. "Hands down. I remember how her stories would paint a picture in my imagination. I'd smell what she wanted me to smell, taste what she wanted to me taste, see what she wanted me to see. Her stories were full of color, dialogue, suspense, and emotion."

Mike is a good storyteller himself. It made sense to me that he'd grown up in a family with an oral storytelling tradition. I didn't give it much thought until a few days later, when I was struggling with a story I wanted to tell a prospect.

Then it hit me. "Oh no," I thought. "I didn't have a grandmother who told me stories like that. I didn't get those bedtime stories. What if you need to be raised on stories in order to become a good storyteller?"

I was shaken—so shaken, in fact, that I left off studying story structure for the time being and began investigating how people actually learn about story. I wanted to know if I'd missed the boat. I wanted to know if I had any hope of ever being a good storyteller.

A few weeks later, I stumbled across an encouraging quote from Daniel Siegel in his book *Mindsight*: "We all make sense of our lives through stories."

I kept reading. It turns out that story building is an intrinsic human process. We are all genetically wired to think in stories—even me.

The difference between Mike and me was, his upbringing had cultivated the storyteller in him, whereas the storyteller in me had been largely dormant all those years—a situation that was no doubt exacerbated by the fact that I'd chosen a career in business, where so much of our training and work is logical and analytical.

But the capacity for storytelling was still inside me. I just needed to discover and nurture my inner storyteller. And thanks to what I'd learned about neuroplasticity—about the brain's constant change and growth, even in adults—I was no longer discouraged. We all have the ability to "rewire" ourselves. I'd been on the right path to start with. With the right help, I could be a good storyteller.

Anybody could.

The Basics of Story Structure

You already know more about story structure than you might think you do. For instance, you probably know—intuitively, at least—that stories have a beginning, a middle, and an end. You know that they have characters and a plot. And you know, from personal experience, that not all stories are created equal. Some stories are simply more moving, memorable, and powerful than others. The secret to building a good story lies in what Edgar Allan Poe called the "unity of effect or impression," where all the elements of a story—characters, plot, setting, emotional tone, and so forth—work together to achieve the story's effect. Here is the Story Leaders framework that will help you build a good story by incorporating all the elements of a story to make your point.

The Point
Start with the point. As Simon Sinek observes in his book, *Start with Why*, we process information from the inside out. His Golden Circle diagram (see Figure 5.2) depicts three

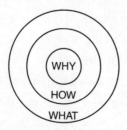

Figure 5.2 Simon Sinek's Golden Circle
Source: www.startwithwhy.com

concentric circles: the inner circle is the *why*; the middle circle is the *how*; and the outer circle is the *what*.

His theory is that the best leaders think and communicate from the inside out, starting with the *why*. Sinek points out that such an approach maps directly to the processing of the mind from the inside out: everything starts with the limbic system (the emotional brain) and goes outward to the neocortex (the thinking brain).

So it makes sense that as sellers, we should organize the ideas we want to communicate to buyers from the inside out. The inside (the *why*) is a belief. Before you build a story, what is the *why* of the story? Or in story terms, what is the *point* of the story? Before you build a story, ask yourself, "What point do I want to make?" A point *is* a belief—the why.

For instance, you might want to make a point such as: *Believe in yourself. Never give up. Good conquers evil. Don't judge a book by its cover. There is a better way.* The point you want to make will depend on your specific sales situation, which we'll discuss in Chapter 6.

The bottom line is, if you don't have a point, you don't have a story. We've had workshop participants tell us, "I've told stories before, but I never thought about making a specific point. Now that I think about the point I am trying to make ahead of time, I'm a much better storyteller."

Setting

Complication

Turning Point

Resolution

Figure 5.3 The Elements of a Story

Once you know what point you're trying to make, you can build a story that makes the point. The other basic components of story we teach in our workshops are defined here and shown in Figure 5.3.

The Setting

The *setting* is the beginning of the story, including its time, location, and any relevant context or conditions (e.g., weather, business, politics, and so on). The setting also provides the introduction to the characters. Every story, even a short story, has at least one character. The setting sets up the journey— how it begins.

The Complication

The *complication* encompasses most of the events of the story and how they complicate the lives of the characters as they face challenges and conflict. Without a struggle, there is no plot; without a plot, there is no story. Sometimes it's an external struggle, between characters or between a character and outside forces, and sometimes it's an internal struggle, a character in conflict with herself as she tries, for instance, to resist a destructive urge or to stick to her principles. In all cases, the complications reveal a character's vulnerability and may include "dumbass moments" like we discussed in Chapter 3.

Often, a character's vulnerability involves shame. If you're telling a story about yourself, owning up to your shame takes a lot of courage. It's worth it, though. When you reveal your shame, your listener will connect with your human imperfection. In this way, having the courage to reveal shame reflects what Daniel Goleman calls "emotional intelligence," which is characterized by self-awareness, social awareness, and effective relationship management.

The Turning Point

The *turning point* is the emotional peak of the story, where the character has an aha moment, a change in perspective, or a change in direction. Things come to a head when a character makes a decision or takes an action that changes the anticipated outcome of the story.

The Resolution

The *resolution* is the final outcome of the story, the untangling of events that reveals how the complication is addressed. Think of the setting as "before" and the resolution as "after."

Story Building

Remember Robert McKee's definition of story: "Story expresses why and how life changes." Building stories is the process of putting language around why and how life changes.

If we map the elements of a story onto the arc, we get a visual representation of a traditional story plot (see Figure 5.4).

A successful story needs a plot that shows change, but it also needs something else: emotional impact. Stories that are too factual lack emotion and therefore lack the power to influence change. Stories that are too emotional lack coherence and don't make sense. In the following pages, we'll tackle the process of story building in two parts that will integrate and balance left- and right-brain processing. First, we'll show you how to use the Story Leaders card system to build stories that follow the arc of change. Then, we'll explain how to give your stories emotional impact.

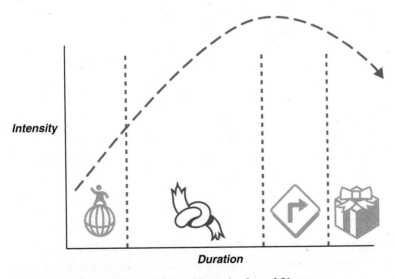

Figure 5.4 The Elements of Story Along the Arc of Change

Part I: The Story Leaders Card System

When we teach story building in our workshops, we story-board our ideas using colored index cards to represent the structural elements of a story. We've found that the different colors (yellow, red, green, white, and blue) help people remember the elements better than if we used white index cards. By the end of the workshop, participants even start speaking in card colors: "I love my yellow card, but I'm still struggling with my white card." For the purposes of this book, we'll be using the icons in Figure 5.3 to represent the different cards. You can purchase your index cards at any office supply store, and you can download our template from the Story Leaders website that will allow you to print out a "storyboard" in color. Just visit www.StoryLeaders .com/downloads and click on "Download Storyboard."

The goal of the card system is to help you build stories one structural element at a time (see Figure 5.5). The cards ensure that your story has all the necessary "ingredients" and are intended to serve as a storyboard, not a script. The idea is to make brief notes and/or bullet points to jog your memory when you practice it aloud later. Think of the cards more as a map of your story, a lightweight framework, not as the story itself.

No need to worry about good grammar or complete sentences. You don't want the language center of your left brain getting in the way. For the same reason, we also encourage you not to build your stories on a computer. When you write by hand, you are using your right brain, which is connected to your five senses and to your emotional brain. When you're typing on a computer, your left brain—with its built-in spell checker and grammar police—is more likely to interfere.

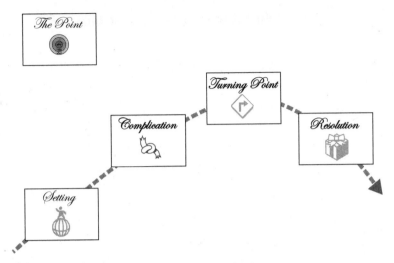

Figure 5.5 How the Cards Correspond to the Arc

For the sake of coherence, we have found that it's best to build a story by working backward, in the following order:

1. The *point* of the story (yellow)

2. The story's *resolution* (red)

3. The story's *setting* (green)

4. The story's *complication* (white)

5. The story's *turning point* (blue)

Starting with the point might seem counterintuitive at first, but it's really not. Our brains don't store memories in chronological order. Rather, memories are filed according to the meaning and emotions we associate with them. By working backward, we're building stories in the same way that our brains organize and recount memories.

(Re)building Ben's Story: John Scanlon

Remember Ben's story about John Scanlon at the beginning of Chapter 1? It's a story that helps explain what led Ben to question our old model of selling and, ultimately, what led to the book you're now holding in your hands. For the purposes of illustration, we're going to "rebuild" that story here using the cards.

 ### Yellow Card: The Point of the Story

The first thing to ask yourself as you begin building a story is, "What's the point?" What is the moral? What belief do you want to communicate? What is the *why*? The yellow card represents the point of your story. In Ben's story about John Scanlon, Ben's point is, "There is a better way to influence a buyer to change."

 ### Red Card: The Story's Resolution

The story's resolution is its ending—the part of the story that drives home your point.

In the John Scanlon story, the resolution comes when the CIO agrees to do the deal. Ben sits there in confusion, astonishment, and embarrassment, having witnessed John build connection and trust with the CIO.

Another example: Suppose you want to make the point that you are trustworthy—your yellow card. So you look back on your life for a story that illustrates that point. You remember a time when you returned a wallet you found in a taxicab in New York, a wallet that contained a substantial sum of money. You now have the ending of the story. Jot it on your red card.

 ## Green Card: The Setting

The green card represents the story's beginning. It's the setup: When and where does the story take place? Who are the characters (e.g., the hero)? What sets the action in motion? And what background information is needed to provide context for the story?

Ben's story about John Scanlon takes place in 2008 after a CustomerCentric Selling workshop, when Ben is invited by his student Jason to observe a sales call. The main characters are Ben, Jason, John, and the CIO buyer. What sets the action in motion is John's unexpected presence at the meeting. The context includes the fact that Ben has trained everybody in the company except John, and that he's looking to "showcase his stuff" during this particular meeting.

Building stories can be difficult, but life is kind to storytellers in that it often presents natural beginnings and endings. Take advantage of them. In Ben's story, Jason's invitation during the sales training workshop provides a natural beginning. In the story about returning a wallet, the natural beginning would be finding the wallet.

Providing context for a story is also critical. Compare these two story settings for a story about a service call.

1. "It was late Friday afternoon when we got a service call from our biggest customer. Their system was down, and they were losing money by the minute . . ."

2. "Last summer, our engineers were almost burned out. They'd just released a new product after months of hard work and overtime. Our lead engineer, Robert, had told the guys they could leave early, and everybody was relaxed and happy, looking forward to a long holiday weekend with no deadline looming. Then we got this call . . ."

The second setting is much more powerful because it provides more context, so we have a better understanding of what's at stake. We also get a sense of the engineers as human beings we can relate to. Compare that to the first beginning, which offers little in the way of context or characters.

In order for a listener to care about your story, he or she has to care about the people in it. Take Ben's story, for example. We care about what happens in the sales meeting because we've "met" Ben and appreciate his situation—his pride in his teaching, his desire to "showcase his stuff." We've also met and care about Jason, who is so confident about what he learned in the workshop that he invites his instructor to observe him in action.

Providing context is important, but be careful not to overdo it, or it can bog down the story. Ben's story is about 850 words long. He establishes the setting and gets the action under way very efficiently—in about 100 words. But if he'd spent another paragraph or two going on about what happened *before* the Scanlon meeting, we might have lost interest before he ever got there. It's a matter of proportion. Ten or 15 pages of setting at the beginning of a 300-page novel isn't unreasonable, but you don't have that kind of leeway when telling a story to a prospect.

White Card: The Story's Complications

Complications are the obstacles and challenges that a character faces between the story's beginning and its turning point (or "climax"). Complications are what make our stories interesting. They create tension and suspense through conflict. Sometimes the conflict is external—between characters, or between a character and outside forces—and sometimes it's internal, a character in conflict with himself. In the story about the wallet, for example, the absence of ID would represent an external conflict where circumstance complicates the hero's efforts to return the wallet. If the hero is tempted to keep the money for himself, that would represent an internal conflict pitting the hero's desires against his values.

Stories in which you, as the main character, are in conflict with yourself can be especially powerful because they present an opportunity to share your imperfections and reveal your vulnerability—which, as we know from Chapter 3, is our most powerful way of getting another human being to open up to us. Stories with characters who lack vulnerability tend to be less compelling. A story about a do-gooder who finds a wallet and returns it with no hesitation isn't nearly so interesting—or so human—as a story about an otherwise good person who is nonetheless strongly tempted to keep the money. Likewise, in our service call example, a story of a superhuman tech support effort will have much less impact than one in which you acknowledge that your firm made mistakes but then you made good on your promises.

Remember, no one connects with perfection. Portray yourself as human, vulnerable, and flawed like the rest of us. The character (you) should be someone the listener can relate to and sympathize with, someone who is not immune to having a "dumbass moment" now and then. This is a phrase we use in our workshops to refer to our own screw-ups, moments when we make mistakes or are resistant to change. In the wallet story, the dumbass moment is when you let yourself get seduced by the money and start thinking about all the great stuff you're going to buy.

In Ben's story about John Scanlon, the complications begin when the prospect doesn't respond well to Jason's sales pitch: "Within minutes, the call flipped: Jason was no longer the one asking the questions. The CIO had taken over the interrogation, and Jason was responding by talking about *what* his products do, the very thing we try to avoid early in a conversation." Ben's dumbass moment comes when he interjects himself into the sales meeting, using a traditional selling model—only to crash and burn.

 Blue Card: The Story's Turning Point

The turning point (or climax) is often the most difficult element for beginning storytellers to pinpoint. There's a tendency to think of the ending as the turning point. For example, in the service call story, a novice might think the turning point is when the customer's issues are resolved. Actually, that would be part of the resolution, along with the customer's reaction to the level of service. The actual turning point would come when, one after another, the engineers volunteer to stay late and work on the problem.

In the wallet story, the turning point isn't when you give the wallet back to its owner. Rather, it's the moment you decide not to keep it because you once had your own lost wallet returned to you, or because you consider how you'd feel if it were your daughter's wallet, or whatever the case may be.

To locate the turning point in a story, *look for a key decision, event, or action*, the moment when the main character changes the expected outcome of the story. In Ben's story, the turning point comes when John speaks up in the meeting—and proceeds to save the day with his storytelling.

Storyboard

Once you have all the structural elements of a story, it's time to create a visual representation of the plot by arranging the cards in chronological order (see Figure 5.6).

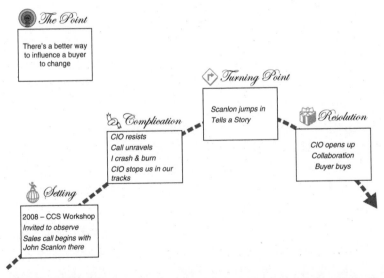

Figure 5.6 How to Lay Out Your Index Cards (John Scanlon Storyboard)

Part II: The Language of Emotion

Up until now, we've focused on the left-brain part of story building: mapping out the structure, making it coherent. Now comes the right-brain part: developing the story's emotional dimension. Think of it as taking your story from 2-D to 3-D.

Our goal is to tell stories that move the heart, not just the head. Stories that lack an emotional impact get labeled by the brain as unimportant. There is a direct correlation between emotional intensity and memory. The experiences we remember best and longest are the ones that have a profound emotional impact on us—for example, experiences that really make us feel good, or experiences that really hurt us. Not only will emotion allow you to move the heart, it will also enable you to *tell* your story from the heart.

The power of emotion in story is reflected in the following old Jewish parable.

Truth and Story

A long time ago in a small village lived two girls, one named Truth and one named Story. Each wanted to be the most popular girl in the village. Soon a rivalry developed between them. They decided to settle the question once and for all with a contest. Each girl would walk through the village. Whichever girl was greeted by the most villagers would be the winner.

Truth went first. She set off down the cobblestone street, passing through the heart of the village. Not one person came out to greet her. By the time she reached the other end of town, she was devastated.

Story went next. She had taken only a few steps before people began coming out of houses and shops. "Story, how are you?" "Story, good to see you!" And so it went until she had passed through the village and reached Truth, who was in tears.

"Story," said Truth, drying her eyes. "You win. You are the most popular girl in the village. Everyone likes you. But why?"

Story put her arm around Truth's shoulder. She spoke in a consoling voice. "You and I," she said, "we are not so different. I have Truth in me, too. But nobody wants to hear the naked truth."

"So what am I supposed to do?" said Truth.

"Here," Story said, removing her cloak. "Take this, and wrap yourself in it."

"What is it?" Truth asked.

"Emotion," Story said. "Wear it, and you, like me, will become Story."

From 2-D to 3-D

Dr. Jerome Bruner observes that stories entail two levels of narrative: (1) the external narrative of a sequence of events, which involves left-brain processing, and (2) the internal mental and emotional narrative of the characters, which involves right-brain processing. At this stage, you've built the first level, but your storyboard is still little more than a map, literally a two-dimensional representation of a story. Now we want you to look at the story and figure out *how you feel about it*. Put some energy into developing the emotional life of your characters. In doing so, you'll be adding a figurative third dimension—emotion.

This part of the chapter is a lot shorter than Part I, but don't be fooled. Putting language around emotion can be really difficult. For one thing, most of us, particularly males, just aren't used to doing it. In our left-brain schooling and jobs, we're encouraged as often as not to *avoid* bringing emotion into the equation.

Fortunately, there are approximately 6,000 words in the English language that represent emotion. The language of emotion is there for the taking. Consider this small sample:

aghast	engaged	positive
angry	envious	proud
annoyed	excited	relaxed
appalled	frightened	reluctant
apprehensive	furious	sad
ashamed	grateful	scared
betrayed	happy	seething
bewildered	horrified	shocked
bored	insecure	stressed
cheated	intrigued	tense
confident	irritated	terrible
conflicted	jaded	terrific
confused	jealous	terrified
cross	keen	triumphant
defeated	lazy	unhappy
delighted	lonely	upset
depressed	lucky	victimized
disappointed	maternal	victorious
ecstatic	negative	wonderful
embarrassed	nonplussed	
emotional	overwhelmed	

The next step is to write down emotions at the bottom of each of your cards, excluding your yellow card (the point). The emotional journey within a story is what *delivers* the t, what will make the listener remember your story, what gives it its impact. In this sense, the real meaning of your story is embodied in its emotional dimension. That's the part that has the power to influence change.

Start with your green card (setting). Ask yourself, "How did I [or the character] feel at this point in the story?" Name the emotion. Now jot it down, just a word or two at the bottom of the card. Feel free to use the preceding list to help you find the words. If the emotion was strong, write the word in big letters or in caps. If the emotion was less intense, write the word smaller. (Remember, the cards are a visual representation of your story. The more visual aspects you incorporate, the more readily your visual right brain will soak it up and remember it.) For good measure, circle the emotion word. Now repeat the process with your white card, then your blue card, and then your red card.

Ben's storyboard appears again in Figure 5.7, this time with emotions added at the bottom of the cards.

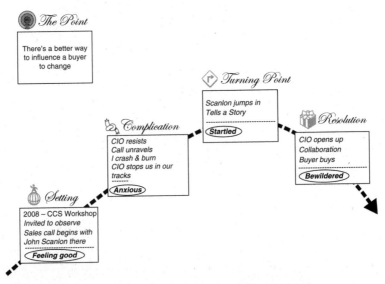

Figure 5.7 Ben's Storyboard with Emotions Added to Cards

The Natural Story Builder in You

The process of building a story using the cards might seem left brain and mechanical. For most people, applying any new framework is uncomfortable at first. What feels unnatural and complicated becomes, through practice and repetition, fluid, even second nature. And with story building, it is human nature to think in story. We're intrinsic story thinkers. The cards do what good storytellers do intuitively—they shape experiences into stories. It's not like you've never done this before. You've been doing it all your life, just not as consciously. With a little practice, you'll be doing the whole process in your head, on your mental index cards. In the workshop, we find that people quickly pick up the card system and after a few stories can visualize the cards and build their stories in real time. It's really just a matter of recounting events and imbuing them with the language of emotion: "What changed? Why? How did I feel?"

CHAPTER 6

Stories for Selling

[
People who tell the stories rule the world.

—Plato
]

Believe What I Believe

Selling isn't just a matter of getting buyers to purchase goods and services. On a more fundamental level, it's about influencing people to change—influencing them to believe what you believe. This isn't just what great salespeople do; it's also what effective leaders, teachers, politicians, coaches, and lawyers do.

Who are the greatest leaders in American history? When we ask this question in our workshops, Abraham Lincoln is always one of the first names we hear. As a leader, Lincoln more than had his work cut out for him. Imagine trying to sell abolition to a nation that was in large part economically dependent on slavery. Imagine trying to hold a nation together even as it sank into a civil war.

Fortunately, Lincoln was a renowned communicator, a skilled orator and writer who understood the power of story. "Instead of berating the incompetent generals who blundered in the Civil War's early battles," writes author Jeff Beals on his blog, "Lincoln educated and motivated them by using stories. To smooth over ruffled political feathers with members of Congress, Lincoln would pull out a story and use it to establish common ground."

Lincoln himself was very conscious of the power of story to "sell" his ideas and beliefs. Here he is in his own words, quoted in *Lincoln on Leadership: Executive Strategies for Tough Times* by Donald T. Phillips:

> *I believe I have the popular reputation of being a story-teller, but I do not deserve the name in its general sense, for it is not the story itself, but its purpose, or effect, that interests me. I often avoid a long and useless discussion by others or a laborious explanation on my own part by a short story that illustrates my point of view. So, too, the sharpness of a refusal or the edge of a rebuke may be blunted by an appropriate story, so as to save wounded feelings and yet serve the purpose. No, I am not simply a story-teller, but story-telling as an emollient saves me much friction and distress.*

Politics is certainly not the only profession in which leaders sink or swim based on their ability to influence others with stories that serve a purpose. In the legal profession, lives often hang in the balance as lawyers attempt to bring judges and juries around to their way of thinking. Consider the infamous O. J. Simpson trial. In 1995, Robert Shapiro's legal defense team stunned the world by convincing a jury that O. J. Simpson was not guilty of murdering his ex-wife, Nicole Brown, and her friend Ronald Goldman.

How did they do it? As Shapiro explains in his book, *The Search for Justice: A Defense Attorney's Brief on the O. J. Simpson Case*, the defense team began the trial by "launching into a relationship with the jury"—a relationship that was established using story, starting with a riveting opening statement. The defense team proceeded to reconstruct the story of O. J. Simpson's life in the hours leading up to the murder. Evidence played a role in the story, but so did emotion—what Simpson was thinking and feeling. The lawyers even brought in passengers who'd been on the same flight as Simpson to describe his emotional state prior to arriving in Los Angeles on the day of the murders. In short, the defense team knew that they needed to humanize Simpson, and they knew that story would be the most effective way to do this.

Ben's Story: "What Are You Talking About?"

After I read Shapiro's book, I gave him a call. I wanted to ask him about his use of story as a way to influence juries to believe what he needed them to believe. Unfortunately, I made the mistake of telling him right off the bat that I'd read his book about the O. J. case—the same book in which he mentions his disdain for interviews about the O. J. case.

"What do you want to know?" he said, already impatient.

I started to tell him that I believed storytelling was underused in our society, but he cut me short.

"Underused?" he said. "What are you talking about? There's nothing 'underused' about storytelling. It's exactly what we do in the courtroom. It's what we've always done."

Before I could get another word in, the conversation got interrupted and Shapiro said he had to go. The call had lasted barely two minutes. I was disappointed I didn't get more time with him. I'd been hoping to interview him. Instead, it basically felt like he'd said those of us in the corporate world are idiots.

It wasn't until that night, as I was telling my wife about the call, that it hit me: Shapiro had told me everything I needed to know. His basic message was, "Maybe you geniuses in corporate sales haven't figured out the power of storytelling yet, but the legal profession has—a long time ago."

And he was right.

Stories for Selling

Whether you're promoting an idea, a belief, a point of view, a product, or a service, the goal is the same—to influence others to believe what you believe. It's all a form of selling.

In this chapter, we're going to discuss how stories can help you sell and how to figure out what types of stories you'll need in your repertoire. The process begins by considering your customers' buy cycle. At the end of the chapter we'll present four real-life "stories for selling" and illustrate how they were composed using the story-building techniques from Chapter 5. We'll close by discussing the particular challenges of prospecting and explain the best way to use a story when you have only seconds to pique a stranger's curiosity.

Mike's Story: Getting Buyers to Open Up

When I began selling first-generation MRP systems in 1975, I had no formal sales training, but I had put in more than 7,500 hours helping our customers at Xerox Computer Services use our integrated set of hosted business software applications to run their businesses. Specifically, I helped people such as controllers, payroll managers, accounts payable supervisors, chief financial officers, and materials managers do their jobs better.

Over time, I came to know the most common needs of these and other specific positions in manufacturing companies. So when I met a new prospect, I'd tell a story about how I'd helped someone else with the same job title, what that person went through, and how she addressed her needs using our system. It was one type of story that almost always got the buyer to open up and share her issues with me: "Hey, I'm in a similar situation myself. . . ."

The only reason I used a story is because, with no formal sales training, that's all I had. I'd previously worked the customer help desk, so I knew all of our customers' stories—practically every imaginable issue and the ways our systems had helped resolve them. Using the stories was simply intuitive.

Unfortunately, I didn't make a point of using stories after the initial sales call, and the rest of the sales cycle tended not to be as smooth or predictable. I didn't realize at the time how valuable the stories were. I thought a story was merely a starter, a way to get someone to open up. Knowing what I know now about how people respond to stories, I think about some of my old prospects and imagine how much more successful I would have been if I'd used stories throughout the entire sales cycle.

Stories with a Point

Think about the stories you already tell in your personal life and the points of those stories. Most of us have some humorous stories in our repertoire—stories we use to break the ice at parties, to make people laugh. Maybe there are other stories you tell as a way of offering advice to friends. Maybe you tell some stories that function as cautionary tales, intended to help people not make the same mistakes you've made. If you have kids, you likely tell bedtime stories. And probably there are stories that you tell simply to make a point.

In building an inventory of stories to influence buyers, we want you to make sure that all of your stories have a point. A good way to start is by considering your customer's buy cycle. What are the steps, or gates, your buyer goes through that lead to a buy decision? A buy cycle might include any number of steps, depending on the particulars of your industry, the size of the potential sale, the length of your customer's buy cycle, how many people are involved in the decision-making process, the complexity of what they're looking to change, and so on.

The Buy Cycle

As part of the original SPIN research project at Xerox, Neil Rackham studied the behaviors of buyers over time. The research pointed to a set of priorities buyers typically need to address and how these priorities take on various degrees of importance throughout the buy cycle. Figure 6.1 is an adaptation based on his study of the buy cycle.

Early in a buy cycle, the number-one priority in the mind of the buyer is his or her needs. Once a buyer has acknowledged a set of needs, he then shifts to phase II, in which the priority becomes evaluating how to address those needs (the details). And once a buyer considers all the options and determines how to address his needs, he

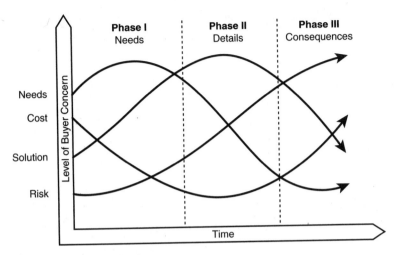

Figure 6.1 The Buy Cycle

moves into phase III, the decision to take action, to jump or not to jump into the lifeboat. Notice that as the buy cycle progresses, the risk of change becomes increasingly signifi-cant in the mind of the buyer, ultimately ranking as the top priority in phase III. This buy cycle occurs universally; however, depending on the complexity of the product or the magnitude of change involved, there can be multiple decision points in each of the three phases.

Sample Buy Cycles
The following are a couple of real-life buy cycles.

Business-to-Business Buy Cycle Here's a long buy cycle in a B2B selling environment. The client is a large enterprise software company. The average sales cycle is six months, and the average sale is $250,000, sold to a committee of buyers.

1. The buyer becomes curious about a new approach.
2. The buyer expresses a set of needs.

3. The buyer is willing to brainstorm new ways with someone he trusts.
4. The buyer sees a new way (the solution).
5. The buyer must get a committee of others to agree to consider change.
6. The buyer understands the value of the new way versus the cost of maintaining the status quo.
7. The buyer sees a path to implement.
8. The buyer makes a decision to act, to sign, to commit.

In reverse order, the steps of a buy cycle can be thought of as the rungs of a ladder, where the top rung represents the decision to buy (see Figure 6.2).

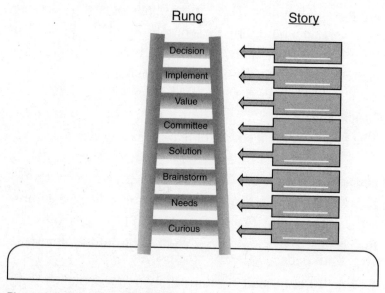

Figure 6.2 Enterprise Buy Cycle

B2C Story Ladder example

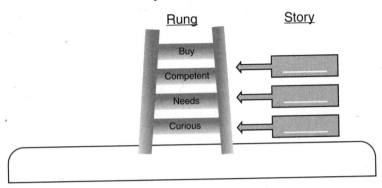

Figure 6.3 Business-to-Consumer Buy Cycle

Business-to-Consumer Buy Cycle Here is a buy cycle we helped another client develop—a financial firm that sells in a business-to-consumer (B2C) environment. The firm sells investment services in a highly competitive marketplace and typically wins new clients in a single meeting (see Figure 6.3).

1. The buyer expresses curiosity.
2. The buyer expresses needs.
3. The buyer achieves confidence that the advisor is competent and trustworthy.
4. The buyer agrees to buy.

The Story Ladder

The goal of sellers at the B2B enterprise software company was to influence buyers to progress through the eight steps shown in Figure 6.2, one rung at a time, culminating with a decision to buy. It's like a pilot flying across the country.

The pilot doesn't simply set his navigation system to go from Los Angeles to New York. Rather, he uses a set of vectors, flying from point to point in order to avoid getting off course.

Think about what your buyer's vectors would be—the rungs on the ladder. Each rung represents a belief or idea your buyer must arrive at before proceeding up the ladder to the next rung in his or her buy cycle. In this chapter, you'll begin to identify an inventory of stories whose points will guide your buyer to the desired belief or idea at each rung.

In order to make use of a story ladder, you will need to build an inventory of stories that help you deliver each of the points you want to make—points that correspond to each rung in your customer's buy cycle. The stories will help your buyer open up and talk about those points. For instance, a story about needs is designed to help the buyer share his needs; a story about solving a problem for another buyer would encourage the buyer to talk about the best solution for his particular problem; and so on. The key is to ask yourself at each rung, "What point do I need to make at this stage in the buy cycle?"

Connection and Trust

If a buyer works for a company that has a procurement process, she's going to be looking at multiple vendors. The expectation is that she will logically consider all of the variables and make the best buying decision—a left-brain decision. At least that's how we always thought it worked. But research now tells us that the very act of saying yes—of saying, "I trust you, I like you, I'm going to take a leap of faith and do business with you"—is in fact a right-brain activity. In other words, buyers *don't* necessarily make logical decisions. More likely, a buyer makes an emotional decision to say yes to the vendor she trusts—the one with whom she has formed the strongest emotional connection—and then she justifies that decision with logic after the fact.

Therefore, a seller's first and foremost goal should be to make an emotional connection with a buyer. Years after his sales stint at Xerox, Mike finally "got" why his intuitive approach had worked so well. Using the power of story, he had been forging emotional connections with his clients.

In almost all selling situations, the first question buyers ask themselves is, "Do I trust this person, or is she like every other salesperson?" In the examples shown in Figures 6.2 and 6.3, the first two rungs of the story ladder are (1) curiosity, and (2) needs. If buyers don't trust you, they aren't going to be curious about what you're selling, and they aren't going to admit their needs to you. (We'll talk more about curiosity later in the chapter.)

Because curiosity, connection, and trust are so essential in almost all sales cycles—whether it's a B2B enterprise sales cycle or a B2C "one-call close"—we believe sellers should have a minimum of three basic story types in their repertoires:

1. Who I Am story
2. Who I Represent story
3. Who I've Helped story

Real-Life Examples

Here are four real-life stories—plus the stories behind the stories. We've also included the storyboard each seller developed using the Story Leaders card system explained in Chapter 5.

The Who I Am Story

The Who I Am story is about your journey—how you ended up here today. The point of the story is to demonstrate why you are doing what you're doing. The resolution of this story is what you currently do and should illustrate the point. Once you have the resolution, you will find a natural beginning. Then search out your complication(s) and turning point.

Linda's Who I Am Story It was the first day of the Story Leaders workshop, and we'd come to the exercise where we were supposed to write our Who I Am story. At first I thought, *I can write a simple story about myself. This should be pretty easy.* But as soon as I put pen to paper, I froze. I had nothing. I started to freak out. The minutes were ticking by, and everyone else in the room was writing. Eventually, I just forced myself to start writing. At the end of the allotted time, by some miracle, I had a story. It was about why I went into sales and how I'd always been a person who cared about my customers.

The next thing I knew, Ben was asking me to share my story. My heart started racing. *Why me?* I thought. *Why are you asking* me? But I didn't want to look like a baby, especially with my vice president in the room, so I did it. I told my story. Basically, I said I'd gone into sales because I'd always cared about my customers and really wanted to do what was best for them. I described myself as a solution-based customer advocate, et cetera, et cetera. As I was telling the story, I realized it wasn't any good. There was no transformation, no lesson learned, no complications, and no dumbass moment. It wasn't a Who I Am story so much as a Why I'm So Great story. I hadn't intended it that way; that's just how it turned out.

I expected Ben to tell me the story needed a little work and then move on to the next person. Instead, he took me back to the very beginning of the exercise.

"What's the point of your story?" he said.

"I guess the point is that I care. I believe my role is to be an advocate for customers."

"Okay," he said, "and what's the red card, the resolution?"

"That I have all these years of expertise and I'm here to serve the customer."

"How about the green card, the beginning of the story?"

"I started in technical training," I said. "I wanted to get into sales because I thought I could have a bigger impact."

"All right. We have the point, the beginning, and the end. So now it's just a matter of figuring out the complications and the turning point."

I avoided looking at my VP. "I didn't really have a complication in my journey."

"Really? You've always been a great customer advocate, from day one?"

"I don't know," I said. "I guess I didn't really have the confidence when I first got into sales."

"Keep going. Tell me more."

"Actually, for several years, I felt people didn't respond to me. I felt that buyers held me at bay. I got a lot of resistance from them."

"Why do you think that was the case?" Ben asked.

"I'm not sure. I remember feeling insecure about it, though. In fact, I used to wear glasses to make myself look smarter. I worried a lot about my clothing, whether I looked the part. I was focusing on my own insecurities so much that it blocked me from being authentic and focusing on my customers. Pretty ironic, huh?"

"How did buyers respond?"

"I didn't feel like I was connecting with buyers," I said. "There was always a barrier. I wasn't serving my customers the way I wanted. For years, I guess I was struggling for approval."

"So there *was* a time you weren't the customer advocate you wanted to be?"

Sure enough, there was my dumbass moment. Years of them. "I never thought about it that way until now," I said. "But yes. There's a huge difference between then and now."

"So how did things change?"

"Well, I remember one day when I was on a sales call, I realized that even though I wasn't connecting with the buyer, I completely understood his problem and knew exactly how to help him. And it dawned on me that by then I'd spent thousands of hours with my customers, and I really did know how to help them. I really knew my stuff. That's what gave me the confidence to do what I'd always wanted to do—to stop worrying about my insecurities and start focusing on helping. A huge burden was lifted from my shoulders. I didn't have to fake it anymore. Plus the whole experience made me a more empathetic salesperson."

And there it was—I had my Who I Am story (see Figure 6.4). It was just a matter of using the cards to interrogate my flimsy Why I'm So Great story, to be more honest and self-reflective.

There's more to the story. Fast-forward to one week after the workshop. I was invited to give a corporate-level presentation to a food and beverage company in Southern California. I reached out to a colleague who was going with me and floated the idea of opening the sales call with a story rather than cutting straight to the punch line, like we normally did. No response. I tried to introduce the idea

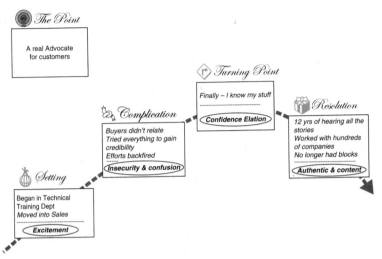

Figure 6.4 Linda's Who I Am Storyboard

again during our internal conference prep call, as we were going over the content, flow, handoffs, and so on, for the presentation. I got a lot of pushback from the lead account manager, who told me it was a bad idea. When he finally let me finish what I was saying, there was dead silence on the line. No one was comfortable with using a story on the sales call. They even decided that I shouldn't be the one in charge of opening the call. I felt defeated, to say the least, and frustrated that I hadn't been able to sell the idea.

When I expressed my frustration to my manager, who had attended the Story Leaders workshop with me, he gave the situation some thought and advised me to do the sales call my way, no matter what anyone else said. He reminded me of one of our colleagues who'd found himself in a similar situation and been vindicated by successfully using a good story. But unlike me, he was a senior vice president.

Even as I drove to the presentation, I was going back and forth about it. *What can the sales team do?* I asked myself.

I'll have the floor. But then: *What if I bomb, and they refuse to ever consider my approach again?*

At the presentation site, our sales team was sequestered in a conference room until our time slot on the agenda. While we were waiting, the six of us did a walk-through of the presentation. Still hoping to sway them, I tried out my story. The team wasn't impressed. "Stick to the script," was their advice. Our time slot was short. We'd been told to get in, do our thing, and get out.

Inside the main conference room sat eight senior executives, from senior VPs to C level. I focused on hooking up my laptop while the account manager quickly ran through introductions. She finished by saying, "Linda is one of our solution architects, and she's going to lead off." I looked up and saw eight men in suits with their arms crossed, leaning back in their chairs, looking like they'd prefer to be doing anything but listening to me. That's when a lightbulb went on in my head: *Tell them my story.*

So I did it—I told them the Who I Am story I'd built in the workshop the week before. Before I knew it, they were uncrossing their arms, leaning in. *Oh my God,* I thought, *it's working!*

The goal of our presentation was to get the clients to reconsider their decision to leave the product lifecycle management (PLM) project. It worked. After I told my story, everyone was more relaxed. The clients opened up and admitted they needed help. We left the conference room that afternoon with their commitment to reengage and clear steps to proceed. And not only had we achieved the results we wanted but the other members of the team complimented me on my delivery, recognizing that my story woke up the executives and had them on the edge of their seats.

The Who I've Helped Story

The Who I've Helped story is about the change that another buyer experienced as a result of buying from you. The point of this story is why he or she chose to buy from you. The resolution of this story is how he or she resolved any earlier complication(s). Once you have the resolution, you will find the natural beginning. Then search out your complication(s) and turning point. Here is one of Ben's Who I've Helped stories about a Story Leaders client.

Ben's Who I've Helped Story: Phil Godwin, Vice President of Sales, Clear Technologies Running a sales organization had proven to be a lot tougher than my client Phil Godwin originally anticipated. A few years ago, Phil's company, Clear Technologies, was a stagnant IBM hardware reseller, and he was a frustrated vice president of sales. His company talked a big game, but they were still those guys presenting "speeds and feeds" and financial justifications in an attempt to upgrade their installed base—and getting nowhere.

When Phil was first promoted to lead his company's sales organization, he implemented Solution Selling, the sales training Mike and I used to offer. He told me it was the only thing he knew to do at the time.

But after the implementation, the majority of his salespeople showed no improvement. In fact, he always had to fight just to get his salespeople to adhere to the sales process; they felt it was more for his benefit than theirs. He could forecast revenues better with the new process because they had pipeline milestones, but their selling behaviors never changed.

In an attempt to differentiate Clear Technologies from every other IT integrator, Phil's company developed its own software offerings: a suite of automated storage reporting tools and security management software.

Still no change in sales.

Essentially, they'd replaced the word *hardware* with the word *solution*, but the way they sold stayed the same. In fact, only Phil's top sellers figured out how to sell these new offerings, while everyone else continued to struggle. He'd really thought that by transforming *what* they sold— combined with the implementation of a sales process like Solution Selling—Clear Technologies would separate itself from all the clutter in the industry. But at the end of the day, nothing really changed. His top few sellers sold a lot, and everyone else remained the same.

Since Phil had been a Solution Selling client, he reached out to us. He shared his story with me, and I shared mine in return—the journey that brought Mike and me to found Story Leaders. At first, Phil was also skeptical. When I suggested he give our workshop a try, he was like, "Yeah, right. More sales training." I remember asking him to tell me about the biggest sale he ever made, what sales process he used. He said he'd had no sales process; it was all about empathy, trust, and connection. That's when he decided to take a leap of faith.

Today, Phil admits it was a big leap for him—a last resort, even. But it was a leap he's glad he took. "We learned how to stop talking about our products so darn much and start communicating with stories—stories of our company, stories of our clients," he told me. "I know that sounds weird, but it's opened up channels I never would have expected. And it's not just storytelling; it's listening to our clients' stories with a real intent to understand. That really has deepened our relationships with clients."

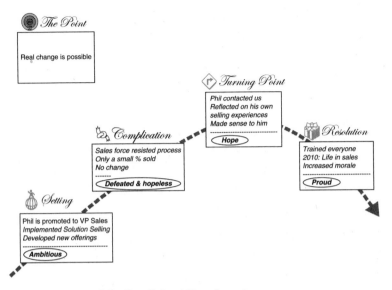

Figure 6.5 Ben's Who I've Helped Storyboard

Another thing that happened, says Phil, was that the employees at Clear Technologies emotionally bought into their company story—that is, once they figured out what the real story was. "We really have changed the company," he said. "I would actually use the phrase 'transformed the business.'" Phil's salespeople began attending Story Leaders workshops in January 2010 and ended up having the biggest year in company history, even in a down economy—43 percent revenue growth in 2010 and in the first quarter of 2011. (For Ben's Phil Godwin storyboard, see Figure 6.5.)

The Who I Represent Story

The Who I Represent story is about the journey of the company you represent. Just as every person has many stories to tell, every company has many stories, especially big companies with a long, complicated history and/or a wide range of

105

product offerings. Resist the urge to present a time line of your company's history. Instead, tell a more specific, focused story. The particular story you choose to tell about your company will depend on the point you're trying to make. The resolution of this story is whatever your company does today that illustrates your point.

Before we train a company's sales force, we like to meet with senior executives to learn the company's story, which in turn becomes a salesperson's Who I Represent story. Such was the case with a client of ours in 2011. Laura, the vice president of marketing, thought it would take about an hour to build her company's story.

"We already know it," she said. "It's on our website on the *About Us* page, and our history and all the key milestones are well documented."

But I'd seen the company history on the website. It was basically a time line, no more a story than the bullet points in Zoe's teacher's history lesson.

"I think it's going to take longer than an hour," I told her. "Can you clear your calendar for the day?"

Sure enough, it took us nearly the entire day. In addition to Laura, we had the vice president of sales, the CEO, and two marketing directors in the room. After some arm wrestling, yelling back and forth, and some black eyes, we finally emerged with a coherent story that conveys the company's guiding beliefs.

"It doesn't just tell *what* we do or *how* we do it," Laura said. "It tells *why* we do what we do. This was the missing piece. I was always frustrated that our salespeople never bought into our story. I realized only now that was because we never communicated our story to them, none of us ever told the story about why we do what we do. We always led with the *what* and the *how*. We just gave them the facts. The new company story that we've developed has inspired our salespeople. Even our veteran reps tell us, 'I never knew what a great company we were.' It's a real David versus Goliath story. It's a story about the underdog. And it not only moves our employees, it moves our clients."

Laura's Who I Represent Story Our story begins in the late 1980s when the Bell System held a monopoly over telephone service in the United States. This is a story about challenging the status quo when the status quo is wrong. At the time, businesses had no other choice for their telecommunications needs. Our founder, an entrepreneur, was frustrated by the situation, especially since Ma Bell's service was so poor. So he set out to challenge them.

He filed an application with the Public Utilities Commission to build out a fiber-optic network in order to offer alternative telecommunications services to businesses. He was turned down. Not once, but several times. He was persistent, and after several more attempts, he was finally granted provisional rights to offer services in a select number of markets to a select number of businesses. Our company was born. Finally the phone company had competition.

Fast forward a few years to the early 1990s. The federal government passed legislation that leveled the playing field for companies like ours. This fueled enormous growth for us, but this growth soon became an Achilles heel. In trying to meet the demands of customers who wanted an alternative to the phone company, we found ourselves trying to service everyone that came to us and we became everything to everyone. To deliver services, we even ended up outsourcing some of our infrastructure back to the phone company.

That's right—we were relying on the company we'd set out to challenge. For a period of time, we lost our competitive edge. Our service suffered and we learned some valuable lessons.

In the early 2000s, we took stock of the situation and decided that in order to provide a real alternative to our customers, and in order to fulfill the founding mission of the company to deliver a real alternative to the phone company, we had to provide a 100 percent independent infrastructure. We invested several hundred million dollars to launch a network build-out and expanded our reach by 300 percent, reducing our dependence on the phone company to zero. We've come out on the other end, fulfilling our founder's belief that there had to be a better way for companies to get telecommunications services. (See Laura's storyboard in Figure 6.6.)

Note: We will present two more examples of Who I Represent stories in Chapter 10 (from a company founder) and in Chapter 11 (from a manager).

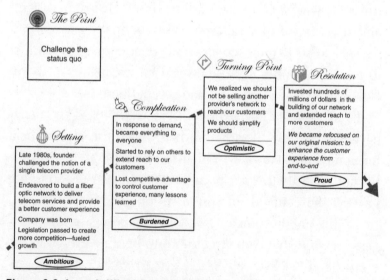

Figure 6.6 Laura's Who I Represent Storyboard

The Right Tool for the Job Story

In addition to the three basic story types (Who I Am, Who I've Helped, Who I Represent), you might find yourself in need of other stories. It's all a matter of figuring out the next point you need to make, the belief or idea your buyer must arrive at before proceeding up the ladder to the next rung in his or her buy cycle. In the following story, Adam Luff, a sales executive for a global enterprise IT company, identified the point he needed to make and built a story that was the right tool for the job.

Adam's Story About a week after I attended a Story Leaders workshop, I gave Ben a call.

"I need help with a story," I said. "But I don't even know which one to use. Can you give me a hand?"

Ben said he'd help, so I told him what my situation was and the point I wanted to make. "I have a call with two IT guys next week—our first meeting—but I don't think my standard Who I Am story is right. And since they've done business with us before, I don't think my Who I Represent story is right, either. I'm stuck."

Then I got to the crux of the matter. "The thing is, these guys are cheap," I said. "They've never spent any money on implementing our applications. They think they can do it all themselves, which is why they've failed three times. Since they already have egg on their faces, I have to tread carefully. I have to get them to realize that doing this project-on-the-cheap is false economy, without ticking them off."

"So you want them to come clean," Ben said. "You want them to admit that the source of their problem is that they keep trying to go it alone—and you want them to trust you enough to accept your help."

"Exactly."

"In that case," Ben said, "I think you're going to need to go first. Have you ever had a similar experience, a time you tried to 'go it alone' and it backfired?"

Now that Ben mentioned it, I had. In the late nineties, I'd been in the same position as those IT guys. I'd worked in an IT department and was put in change of a software implementation that required me to stitch together three different systems. I didn't have any middleware tools, but I was full of guts and determination. Looking back, I guess I was a bit of a maverick, trying to impress everybody by doing it myself without spending any money. In those days, that's how I thought you ran a business. I struggled with the project for about 18 months, practically pulling out my hair and getting more miserable all the while. After yet another meeting in which I'd had to tap-dance around the problem, the CIO took me aside. "Stop being a bloody Rambo," he said, "and get yourself some help." But by then it was too late. I knew he wasn't going to sack me, but I also realized there was no way to save face after failing so badly for so long. So I left. (See Figure 6.7.)

"Sounds like a good story to me," Ben said.

"But there's no resolution," I said.

"In this case," Ben said, "I think that's the point—that you weren't able to resolve the situation, that you failed, that there *was* no resolution. You portray yourself as vulnerable and flawed. I think it's the right tool for the job."

The following week, when I showed up at the client's office, the receptionist led me to the company cafeteria—not exactly an intimate setting for a meeting. The two IT guys were waiting for me. They seemed very defensive, sitting there with their arms crossed, probably expecting the standard chest-beating exercise we salespeople are known for. I started

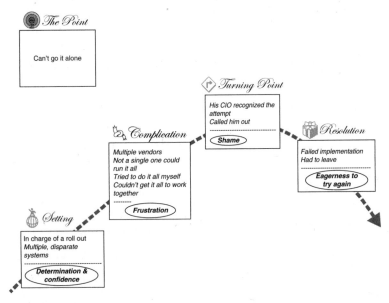

The Point
Can't go it alone

Turning Point
His CIO recognized the attempt
Called him out
- - - - - - - - - - - - - - - -
Shame

Complication
Multiple vendors
Not a single one could run it all
Tried to do it all myself
Couldn't get it all to work together
- - - - - -
Frustration

Resolution
Failed implementation
Had to leave
- - - - - - - - - - - - - -
Eagerness to try again

Setting
In charge of a roll out
Multiple, disparate systems
- - - - - - - - - - - - - -
Determination & confidence

Figure 6.7 Adam's Storyboard

by asking if I could tell them a story. They got a kick out of that. One of them actually did a Wile E. Coyote cartoon double take.

"Sure," he said. "Whatever."

So I started in. When they realized I was telling *my* story, not a company story, they stopped being so standoffish and started paying attention. And sure enough, once I passed the torch, they opened up and told me why the previous implementations hadn't gone so well—exactly what I'd been hoping to hear from them.

But then something happened that I *hadn't* been expecting. One of the guys pulled out his phone, called a coworker, and asked him to meet us in a conference room. When he got there, the IT guy said, "Come meet with Adam. He's not trying to sell us anything. He just wants to hear about what's going on to see if he can help." They eventually called in yet another colleague, and I spent the next two hours in that room, listening to their stories. By the time I was done, I had three real opportunities when all I'd hoped to do was break the ice with the original two guys.

The Curiosity Rung: Prospecting

Whether you're making a cold call, making a warm call, or working the floor at a trade show, approaching strangers for the first time is always tough—probably the toughest part of being a salesperson. The success rate is low. Rejection is a given. It's no wonder so many of us develop a case of "call reluctance."

The key to success, of course, lies in piquing a prospect's curiosity. But we have to be quick. We know we have only a brief window of opportunity—10 to 20 seconds—before a prospect says "tell me more" or "not interested." A lot of salespeople use those few seconds to talk about what they do or how they do it. We believe that's a mistake. Remember Simon Sinek's Golden Circle from Chapter 5 (see Figure 5.2)? Sinek contends that we are most effective when we communicate from the inside out. The inside (the *why*) is a belief. If you have only a few seconds to make a buyer curious, start with the *why* of your story—the point (yellow card). Lead with a belief, not facts. Use those first few seconds to activate someone's curiosity, which will earn you the right to tell the rest of the story.

Let's say Ben is at a trade show cocktail reception with lots of potential prospects. He approaches the vice president of one such company and leads with the point (in italics) of his Who I've Helped story about Phil Godwin: "My name is Ben Zoldan with Story Leaders and although we've never met, I'd love to share a story with you about another senior sales executive I've worked with who believed in *affecting real change; creating a real transformation throughout his organization.*" (See the yellow card of the storyboard in Figure 6.5.)

The VP of sales can go one of two ways: he will either say, "Sure, tell me more," or break eye contact and walk away. We have found that when we offer a story, very few people turn us down. And when we offer a story that is connected with a point (a *why*), we've found it increases the chances of piquing someone's curiosity. When the VP says, "Sure," Ben can then tell a two-minute version of his Who I've Helped story about Phil Godwin.

Leading with the *why* activates the receptive limbic brain, as opposed to leading with the *what* or *how*, which activates the left brain's skeptical defense mechanisms. The outcome or resolution (red card) is the *what* of a story. If Ben had led with the resolution of his Phil Godwin story—"I helped Phil increase revenues by 30 percent"—he would have sounded like every other salesperson. Instead, by working from the inside out, leading with a belief, rather than a *what*, he connected with the VP's limbic brain (the emotional brain), where curiosity resides—and earned a couple more minutes, enough time to tell the rest of the story, which includes the resolution—*what* happened.

Marketers know all about appealing to the limbic brain. Consider Apple's popular and successful "Think different" ad campaign. The commercials don't lead with facts: "An iPad will allow you to do *x, y,* and *z!*" Rather, they present viewers with images, music, and a simple belief ("Think different") that make viewers feel good about Apple products and curious to learn more. As salespeople, we can do the same with our prospects if we lead with belief and emotion and save the facts for later.

CHAPTER 7

The Collaboration: Storytelling and Story Tending

[
To touch the soul of another human being is to walk on holy ground.

—Steven Covey
]

Storytelling

Now that you understand the power of story and have built some stories of your own, it's time to start putting them to use in a collaborative, reciprocal way—in real sales situations. Keep in mind that your stories are merely a means to an end, a way of helping your buyer to progress through his or her buy cycle. Ultimately, the goal is to influence your buyer to believe what you believe, to get to the top rung of the story ladder, to say yes.

The Language of Emotion

The first thing to understand about storytelling is that it's not just *what* you say but *how* you say it. In fact, it's *mostly* how you say it. People tend to think of spoken language as our primary means of communication, but studies suggest that words alone make up only 7 percent of human communication. The other 93 percent consists of tone of voice (38 percent) and nonverbal cues (55 percent) such as facial expressions, gestures, and body posture (see Figure 7.1).

Most researchers now agree that spoken words are used primarily to convey information, via the left brain, whereas our other means of communication (body language, tone of voice, and facial expressions) are used primarily to convey feelings and emotions, via the right brain. "Body language is an outward reflection of a person's emotional condition," write Allan and Barbara Pease in *The Definitive Book of Body Language*. "Each gesture or movement can be a valuable key to an emotion a person may be feeling at the time."

Therefore, if we're going to activate a buyer's limbic brain—his operating system, the part of the brain that decides

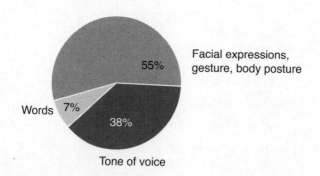

Figure 7.1 How We Communicate
Source: Based on *Active Listening* by Carl Rogers and Richard Farson

to trust, to act, to take a leap of faith and try something new, to *buy*—then we need to be mindful of what Malcolm Gladwell calls "the persuasive implications of nonverbal cues" in his discussion of how the best salespeople influence others in his book *The Tipping Point*.

The system of cognitive transmission from mind to body is far more evolved than from mind to mouth. Long before humans developed spoken language, we were communicating with our bodies. Body language is also how we first begin communicating as infants. An 18-month-old shakes her head back and forth when she's had enough peas, hugs a teddy bear that makes her happy, waves her hands when she's excited.

Studies show that the signals sent by the limbic system to the body are much quicker and more reliable than the transmissions of our left-brain language center. In other words, the body goes first, and the body doesn't lie. Before a five-year-old fibs about raiding the cookie jar, he'll instinctively cover his mouth with his hand. When we feel threatened or defensive, we cross our arms. When we feel shame or embarrassment, we look away. When we feel pride, our chest rises and expands. Emotions such as boredom, excitement, fear, and arousal are readily conveyed by our facial expressions—often whether we want to convey them or not.

When the messages we send are incongruent—when our words don't match our body language—a listener will tend to tune out the words and subconsciously focus on nonverbal cues. For instance, when someone asks how we're doing and we say, "Fine," the way we say it reveals a lot more than the word itself. In fact, your tone of voice and nonverbal cues can even tell a listener the exact *opposite* of what your words are saying. Even when we try very hard to deceive someone, our bodies are likely to give us away. Think of a poker "tell," the unconscious physical gesture that tips off one player to the fact that another player is bluffing.

The power of nonverbal communication is well understood by actors. Silent-film audiences didn't need words to know when Charlie Chaplin was feeling downtrodden and dejected, or when Buster Keaton was determined to succeed. Even with today's movies, you can easily follow the emotional trajectory of the story with the sound turned off.

Nonverbal cues are critical even for orators and singers, people whose performances we strongly associate with the words. Look, for instance, at the lyrics to your favorite pop song. Chances are they don't exactly qualify as poetry. But put them into the mouth of a gifted singer, and suddenly, shallow, simplistic lyrics can become moving, even profound. The effect can be even more dramatic in a live performance, where the singer's body language and facial expressions come into play. Or watch a Martin Luther King, Jr. speech with the sound turned off—no words *or* tone of voice—and you'll still get a strong sense of his power as a speaker and the emotion he wants to convey. It's all in the delivery, using nonverbal communication to put emotion behind words.

Communicating the Emotion of Your Story

The left brain, where the language center resides, specializes in picking up and sending verbal messages. The right brain specializes in interpreting and sending nonverbal messages. Effective storytelling involves integrating the two sides of the brain, using both the verbal and nonverbal languages of emotion. The result is collaborative communication. Our brains are wired to connect with another person when feelings are expressed. The greater the feeling, the stronger the connection.

As Dr. Daniel J. Siegel writes in *Parenting from the Inside Out*:

> When the primary emotions of two minds are connected, a state of alignment is created in which the two individuals experience a sense of joining. The music of our mind, our primary emotions, becomes intimately influenced by the mind of the other person as we connect with their primary emotional states. . . . Resonance occurs when we align our states, our primary emotions, through the sharing of nonverbal signals. . . . When relationships include resonance, there can be a tremendously invigorating sense of joining. (pp. 64–65)

Emotion is contagious. If we want someone else to feel what we're feeling—if we want to trigger their mirror neurons, the basis for reciprocal conversation and reciprocal sharing of emotions—then we need to communicate our emotions through our body language as well as our words.

"Mirror neurons may also link the perception of emotional expressions to the creation of those states inside the observer," writes Siegel. "In this way, when we perceive another's emotions, automatically, unconsciously, that state is created inside us." We may therefore experience fear when we see someone else in a state of fear, we may be inclined to laugh when someone else laughs, and so forth.

The storyboards you built in the last chapter are, quite literally, nothing but words on paper. It's true that you need good stories, and it's true that you need the right story for the job, depending on your selling situation and the rung of the story ladder you're on. But that's not enough. When it comes time to actually tell your stories, to communicate them to another human being, remember that those words on the index cards account for only 7 percent of the information you'll be conveying. The other 93 percent will come from *how* you tell the story, using your tone of voice, facial expressions, and nonverbal cues.

So how do you tell a story with real emotion? Research indicates that our bodies will convey an emotion if we "check in" and become aware of that emotion. That's one of the reasons we ask you to write, at the bottom of each index card, words that represent the emotions associated with each part of the story.

Remember Adam's "Right Tool for the Job" story from Chapter 6 about the dangers of going it alone instead of asking for help? His storyboard is shown again in Figure 7.2.

Chances are, when Adam told his story, he used the words at the bottom of each card to describe the emotion he was feeling at each point in the story: "Back then I had

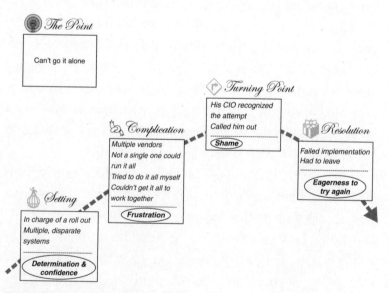

Figure 7.2 Adam's Storyboard

a lot of *determination* and *confidence*. I felt like *I could do it all*. . . . When I wasn't able to integrate the systems, *frustration* set in. . . . After my CIO called me out, I was full of *shame*. . . . I learned my lesson after the fact, and I was *eager to try again*."

But Adam didn't have to use the words. In fact, he could have told the story without using the actual words at all, and if he told it well, emoting fully, the buyer still would have known exactly how he felt throughout the story.

When you tell your stories, be sure to "check in" with your emotion words. Doing so will help you avoid monotone or tone-deaf storytelling. Just seeing the words on paper (or thinking about them when you're telling a story from memory) will trigger cognitive transmissions that activate the right brain. Since the right brain is kinesthetically connected to the rest of the body, those transmissions will make it easier for you to emote. It's that simple: by being aware of and attuned to the emotions, you can communicate them more fully. Your tone of voice, speech rhythms, facial expressions, and body language will reflect the emotion you're recalling. This is storytelling from the inside out, starting with the emotion, not the words. It is a natural, intrinsic process. You might even try acting out parts of your story. Jump in and relive particularly vivid moments. The listener will jump in with you.

Exercise

The next time someone asks how you're doing, say, "Fine, thanks," but send a different message with your tone of voice, facial expression, or body language. Observe how the person responds to you. Which is more convincing to him or her, your words or your other cues?

> **Exercise**
>
> Act out the emotion word at the bottom of one of your index cards. Have a friend try to guess what word you wrote down and tell you why (s)he thinks so. For example: "I think the word was *frustrated*, because you tensed up and hit the table with your fist."
>
> Now tell one of the stories you built using the card system, but don't use the actual emotion words at the bottom of the cards—or any similar words. Have your friend try to guess what words you wrote down. Keep practicing until conveying the emotions in your story comes naturally to you.

Ben's Story: Bill Clinton's Reality Distortion Field

I remember watching with a friend one of the 1992 U.S. presidential debates. It was George H. Bush, Bill Clinton, and Ross Perot in a town hall format, with an audience of ordinary Americans asking the questions. About halfway through the debate, the moderator took a question from a young African American woman in the third row.

"How has the national debt personally affected each of your lives?" she asked.

It was President Bush's turn to answer first. My friend elbowed me. "Did you see that?" he said. "Bush just lost the election."

"What are you talking about?"

"While she was asking the question, he looked at his watch."

Sure enough, the gaffe received a lot of attention after the debate, but it was only the beginning of Bush's mistakes.

"Well," Bush said. "I think the national debt affects *everybody—*"

"No," the woman interrupted. "How has it affected *you personally?*"

Bush looked stumped. After fumbling through an answer that devolved into an analysis of the semantics of the question itself, he took his seat. Bill Clinton followed with what struck me as a much stronger answer, and I came away from the debate feeling that he'd won.

Years later, once I started to learn about the importance of nonverbal communication, I came across what has become a widespread description of Bill Clinton's charisma: "He makes you feel like you're the only person in the room." Commentators have dubbed it Clinton's "reality distortion field." That got me thinking about that 1992 debate, so I found the clip online to see if I remembered it correctly.

Sure enough, Bush's answer seemed stiff, incoherent, cold. And sure enough, Clinton's answer was more sympathetic and direct. But it wasn't the difference in the candidates' answers that struck me; it was the difference in their body language.

I watched the clip several times with the sound off. When Bush rises to answer the question, he hikes his pants like a cowboy facing a bull but takes only a step or two from his chair—like a nervous cowboy. When Clinton rises to answer the question, he immediately crosses the stage and stands near the front row, as close to the woman as he can get. As Bush answers the question, he takes another step forward but tucks a hand in his pocket. His facial expression is almost angry. He repeatedly turns away from the woman to address the rest of the audience. When he manages to look her in the eye, he wags his finger as if he's scolding her. Clinton, on the other hand, speaks directly to the woman as

123

if she's the only person in the audience. His facial expression is sincere and compassionate. His hand gestures—touching his chest with both hands—convey inclusion and warmth. During Clinton's answer, the look on the woman's face makes it clear which candidate connected with her. And the look on Bush's face—mouth open, stunned—makes it clear that he knows he's out of his league.

That four-minute debate clip taught me everything I needed to know about the value of body language and eye contact, the way nonverbal cues contribute to that intangible quality known as charisma. It wasn't about what Clinton said; it was all about how he said it.

Metaphors Shine in the Storyteller's Toolbox

While the actual words you use to tell your story may make up only 7 percent of what you convey to a listener, you still want those words to count. One way to make your language more vivid and full of emotion is through the use of figures of speech such as metaphors.

A metaphor is a comparison that shows how two things that are not alike in most ways are actually similar in a significant way. For instance, the title of this section employs a metaphor, likening figures of speech to tools in a toolbox. You could also think of them as weapons in an arsenal, cards in a deck, and so forth—you get the idea.

A metaphor expresses the unfamiliar or abstract (the tenor) in terms of the familiar and concrete (the vehicle). When Pat Benatar sings "love is a battlefield," *battlefield* is the vehicle for *love*, the tenor. Some common types of metaphors include allegories, parables, and similes. A simile is simply a metaphor that uses the word *like*: she runs like the wind, he drinks like a fish, and so on.

Metaphors are particularly useful for expressing intangible feelings and emotions. Let's say you're telling a story that involves a major deadline at work. You might describe the deadline as a noose around your neck, getting tighter every day. Or maybe it's more like a dark cloud, a black hole, the edge of a cliff, an eighteen-wheeler bearing down on you, or a gun to your head. The range of possibilities is limited only by your imagination.

The power of metaphor lies in its ability to create a visual image in the listener's mind. When a listener has to struggle to interpret or clarify an idea, the skeptical left brain is activated. Metaphors can make your story more colorful and reduce your listener's mental "heavy lifting," keeping him or her in a more receptive right-brain mode.

Getting Started and Passing the Torch

There will be sales situations when you can just launch right into a story as part of the natural flow of conversation. That's how John Scanlon, the CEO whose story is in Chapter 1, did it: "Hey guys, that reminds me of a time when I was at MCI. . . ."

In other situations, you might need to shift conversational gears in order to start your story. There's always the simple, straightforward approach: "Can I tell you a story?" Or maybe your selling situation will allow for a more specific transition: "Mind if I share a story about another CIO?" or, "Can I tell you a story about a client of mine who was facing similar challenges?"

In any case, these are all versions of that age-old story beginning "once upon a time." Don't underestimate its power.

In our experience, people simply don't say no to the offer of a story. For starters, it would be hard to do so without coming off as rude. More important, the promise of a story has a powerful subconscious effect, relaxing the left brain's defenses and heightening the right brain's receptivity. When we hear "once upon a time," we subconsciously tell ourselves, "Oh, it's just a story. I don't have to *do* anything or *decide* anything. I can just listen and enjoy." But at the same time we're relaxing into the story, we also focus and pay attention, because we are story learners, biologically wired to learn through narrative. And so, paradoxically, at the same time our subconscious is saying, "It's just a story," it's also saying, "I'd better pay attention; I might learn something." This, as discussed in Chapter 5, is the power of story.

Meet Them on the Left Side

Most buyers are clutching their wallets when they first meet a salesperson. Their left-brain defenses are on high alert. Before a seller tries to connect with a buyer's right brain, it's a good idea to meet the buyer where they are—satisfy the left-brain first. We recommend beginning sales calls by offering a quick agenda, telling the buyer what your plan is: "What I'd like to do today is start by sharing my story with you. I'm interested in hearing yours too, and then we can decide where to go from there. Sound good?" Offering an agenda can quickly satisfy the buyer's left-brain appetite to know what's going on, which then opens the door for the seller to shift over and begin activating the buyer's right brain with a story.

Of course, there's no one right way to start a sales call. And sometimes it's the buyer, not the seller, who begins the conversation. In those cases, instead of *telling* a story right off the bat, the seller has an opportunity to begin by *tending* the buyer's story—a process described later in this chapter.

How Long Should My Story Be?

The length of a story is an important consideration. You want a story to be long enough—that is, developed enough—that it effectively makes its point. But you don't want it to be so long that the listener begins to feel bored or impatient. Ultimately, the ideal length depends on the story itself. Mark Hurd's story about his daughter, presented at the beginning of Chapter 4, lasted barely two minutes—but in that short time, he managed to transform the room.

The ideal length also depends on how much time you have and on your listener's reaction. If you sense that your listener's attention span is nearing its end, wrap up the story quickly. If your listener looks like he hopes you never stop, milk the story for all it's worth.

It's a good idea to have a mix of shorter and longer stories in your repertoire—30 seconds, 3 minutes, even 10 minutes if, for example, you're making a presentation using visuals. In fact, it's also a good idea to practice shorter and longer versions for each of your stories.

In our experience, a story for a first sales call should take not more than three minutes to deliver effectively. You want to begin establishing an emotional connection with your buyer through story as soon as possible; at the same time, however, you don't want your buyer to feel buttonholed before you've even gotten a chance to know each other.

We'll take up the issue of story length again in Chapter 10 when we get into the tactical use of different stories—how to prospect with a story, how to train using a story, and so on.

Passing the Torch

One of the goals of telling stories in sales situations is to get the buyer to open up and share stories in return. So, when you're done with your story, always remember to pass the torch.

Sometimes, passing the torch involves little more than keeping quiet. With a moment of silence after a story, you create a natural opening in the conversation for your buyer to wade in with one of her or his stories. That's how John Scanlon did it.

But sometimes you'll need to be more proactive, prompting the listener. For example: "Enough about me. How about you?" "So that's how it went with the other CIO. What's *your* story?" "Those are the challenges my last client was facing. I'd be interested to know how it's been for you."

Everyone has a story to tell if given the chance. People *want* to tell their stories—they want to be heard, they want to connect, they want to be understood. It's human nature. Pass the torch to your listeners and watch them run with it.

Story Tending

The idea of "tending" a buyer's story came from a conversation when we reflected on the most memorable sales from our own careers. In each of the stories we shared, the common theme was that we knew the stories of the people who were responsible for making the decisions. We both recounted how we got our then-buyers to open up with us. We thought of words that represented how we got those stories from our buyers. The word *tending* came up. We tend to the things and the people in our lives that are important to us.

If we make the idea of the buyer's story important, we should tend to it. Why then don't salespeople think of the word *tending*?, we asked each other. Isn't it more apt than phrases like "diagnosing a buyer" or "getting their pains"?

Tending implies a completely different mind-set in the way we approach buyers. Rather than being narrowly focused on extracting a buyer's problems or pains, a seller who *tends* a buyer expresses genuine caring and curiosity about the buyer's whole story: where he was, where he is now, how he feels, where he'd like to be in the future and why. In doing so, the seller not only learns everything he needs to know about the buyer's situation but also makes the critical emotional connection that can ultimately lead to the buyer saying yes.

In the workshop, we now ask participants, "What in your personal life do you tend?" Their answers usually include children, spouses, parents, gardens, and so forth—things that grow. We believe relationships and the conversations that foster them should be nurtured the same way. That's what we mean by "story tending"—bringing a sense of caring and purpose to your sales calls and to the stories you and your buyers share.

A big part of story tending involves listening. In the next chapter, we'll discuss the skills that will help make you a great listener. But story tending also involves making choices about which stories to tell. The goal is to help buyers open up and tell their own stories. In this way, storytelling becomes a back-and-forth collaborative process.

Reciprocity and the Story Ladder
If the ultimate goal of our stories is to influence buyers to believe what we believe, then we must get buyers to tell us

their stories in return, to share the information that will help us help them. As a seller, use your stories to go *first*, telling stories that make points and that prompt buyers to tell their own stories on the same subject. Think of yourself as holding the buyer's hand, guiding him up the ladder, letting him know it's safe. One story begets the next, each a means to an end: your buyer's yes.

Adam's Climb Up the Story Ladder

Let's go back to Adam's story about the dangers of *going it alone*. Adam was stuck on a rung where he needed his buyers to acknowledge that they had a problem. Without that acknowledgment, the sale was going nowhere. He determined that the right tool for the job was his personal story about a time when he'd tried to go it alone and failed. After Adam went first and showed his own vulnerability, he passed the torch. His buyers then felt comfortable telling him their story, in which they confessed to being in a similar situation. In this way, the point of Adam's story became the point of his buyers' story, too—they'd moved up to the next rung together. A story begets a similar story.

In a more traditional approach, Adam might have broken out his slide deck or demo, drawing on his corporate product training and offering the buyers his value proposition. But then he'd have run into all the dangers of traditional selling techniques:

○ **We confuse the buyer.** When we launch into detailed descriptions about our products, we force buyers to use left-brain processing to analyze the heaps of data we're sending their way. Of course, the left brain has an unending appetite for information—give it some details, and it has to have more. The sales call quickly devolves into endless product hell.

○ **We create skepticism**. As humans, we are inherently skeptical of other people's positions and opinions. When a seller launches into a sales pitch and starts detailing her value prop, however persuasive or reasonable, she will trigger the buyer's left-brain skepticism and scrutiny. We intuitively know when someone is trying to persuade us, and we instinctively resist it—it's a natural defense mechanism. Also, any emotional connection made earlier in the sales call is likely to be diminished or to fly out the window at that point.

○ **We fail to connect with the key part of the buyer's brain**. Once a salesperson shifts from storytelling to traditional selling, he is trying to move the buyer's head, not his heart. But it's the heart—the emotional limbic system—that makes the decision to say yes. That's the part of the brain that sellers need to be speaking to.

Fortunately, Adam didn't make the mistake of reverting to a pitch. He knew that stories aren't just a way to open up a conversation but that they build on one another throughout a conversation. He also knew storytelling isn't linear or serial—this story, then this one, then this one. Rather, stories can be used in different ways in different situations, depending on the buyer's stories. And so, mindful of tending his buyer's story, he offered a Who I've Helped story about a client of his who had faced similar problems. The point of his story was to show the buyers that their problems could be successfully addressed. He wanted them to understand how he could help them long before he ever had to break out his product information.

"Your situation reminds me of another IT director I worked with," Adam said. And then he told them about Bob, a seasoned 20-year executive who was doing fine until compliance regulations mandated that his company implement a new security application. Given his experience, Bob thought he could handle the job himself, and for several months, things seemed to be going fine. But then it came time for his company to generate its first compliance report since the implementation of the new application. Trying to pull data from the company's disparate systems was a disaster. "So Bob brought us in on a consulting basis," Adam said, "just to put out the fire. But once we helped him integrate the security app across his systems, he realized we had the capacity and the know-how to do the same for *all* his applications. He enlisted our integration professional services, and by using our middleware with open APIs, he was able to make all of his systems work together."

Instead of trying to persuade the buyers that he could solve their problems, Adam used this story about someone else who took a leap of faith and tried a new way. The story gave the buyers a sense of what was possible—a glimpse into their own future if, like Bob, they chose to buy. In this way, Adam was tending their big-picture story, collaborating with them to craft a resolution in which his products and services were the answer to their problems.

Then Adam passed the torch. "Anyhow," he said, "your situation just reminded me of Bob's."

The buyers reciprocated with another story about their failed integration efforts, one that included a more detailed description of what they'd hoped to accomplish. By internalizing Adam's last story, they had begun envisioning a solution to their own problems.

Instead of pursuing the traditional diagnose/prescribe dynamic, Adam had managed to turn the entire sales call into a collaborative sharing of stories. In doing so, he got the full story from his buyers—all the information he needed to figure out what their problems were and how he could help solve them. But instead of using this information to try to persuade the buyers, he kept using it to choose his next story. Each story was used with a purpose—as a means to get the buyers to open up and share a related story. Inviting a buyer to share her or his whole story requires tending, and tending requires real listening, which we'll cover in the next chapter.

Empathic Listening

Are You a Good Listener?

Calvin Coolidge once said, "No one ever listened themselves out of a job." No one ever listened themselves out of a sale, either. But there's a lot more to listening than most people think, and it's a lot harder to do than most people realize. This chapter is about getting people to really open up. Real emotional connections—the kind that can lead to change—are forged when people truly feel listened to. It's something that doesn't happen much in our society in general, much less in sales.

The biggest part of story tending is *listening*. In order to understand our buyers' stories, in order to validate our buyers, in order to figure out what stories we should be sharing in return to move up the ladder together, we must first listen. But if we want to get our buyers' whole stories, we have to do better than what generally passes for listening in our culture. Turn on the Sunday morning news programs and you'll see pundits so eager to spout their views that they hardly seem to hear the other guests, much less listen to them. You can see the same thing, albeit on a less dramatic scale, every day, all around you—on the street, in meetings, at your dinner table, on sales calls, and so on.

Everyone wants the chance to tell his or her story, but it's hard to find someone who will really listen. You probably know the feeling. You're having a conversation, and the minute you say something interesting, the other person jumps in, or starts talking over you. Or worse, the other person isn't paying attention to what you're saying or obviously doesn't care. Isn't it great to talk to that rare person who seems sincerely curious about what you have to say? Who actually lets you talk?

Real listening (what we call "empathic listening") involves support, encouragement, sincere curiosity, patience, and caring. It doesn't come naturally, and it's difficult to do, as it goes against many of our impulses as salespeople—to jump enthusiastically into a conversation on a call, to put our expertise on display, to get to the point, to "rescue" a buyer, and so on. But here's the good news about listening. Even if you think you're a terrible storyteller—okay, even if you *are*—you'll still be better than 95 percent of the salespeople out there if you teach yourself to become a good listener. As an added bonus, you'll likely improve your storytelling in the process. It's a reciprocal relationship: the better listeners we become, the better storytellers we become, and vice versa.

Our goal in this chapter is to give you a new appreciation of the importance of listening and a model of how to do it well. But first, let's look at some of the behaviors that prevent us—especially, in some cases, salespeople—from being good listeners. In order to overcome them, we must first be aware of them.

Listening Blocks

A listening block is a behavior that hinders effective communication by preventing one person from truly listening to another person. Such behaviors include rehearsing what you're going to say next, judging the speaker or her statements, placating the speaker, sparring with the speaker, mind reading, daydreaming, advising the speaker, derailing the conversation, insisting on being right, and so on. Salespeople, by virtue of prevailing sales-training methods, are inclined to fall prey to a particular combination of these blocks, such as the following.

Relying Too Much on Our Ears

Which of your senses do you most closely associate with listening? Not surprisingly, when we ask this question in the workshop, almost everyone says "hearing."

With our ears, we perceive tone of voice, inflection, and, of course, words. But what about the other 55 percent of human communication that comprises facial expressions, gestures, and body language? To "listen" to those forms of communication, we need our eyes. When it comes to listening, our eyes are at least as important as our ears, if not more so. When we rely too much on our ears, we're getting less than half the story.

Dr. Mark Goulston, author of the bestselling book *Just Listen: Discover the Secret to Getting Through to Absolutely Anyone*, learned this lesson the hard way.*

Mark Goulston's Story: Listening into People's Eyes

"You listen into people's eyes," Doc Barham told me.

I said: "What?"

"When you sit down with people, what you first notice is people's eyes, and then you look and listen into them for their hurt, pain, fear, anger, and terror, and when you do, they share whatever it is with you. And then they exhale, feel relieved, and open themselves up to you. That is your secret sauce," he explained.

Doc Barham is CEO of Xtraordinary Outcomes, a company that identifies what makes individuals, companies, and organizations extraordinary and, in doing so, helps them to come from that special "tipping point" place to become even better. He had been interviewing me about how I work with patients and seem to be able to get through to some of the toughest ones.

Like many "talents" or skills that people have, it was spawned out of a terrible experience that taught me it. I hadn't made the connection until Doc identified the way that I listen.

Nearly 30 years ago, I had one of the most awful experiences in my career as a psychiatrist. I had been paged to go up to a patient's room at UCLA Medical Center to "okay" the soft restraints the surgeons had placed on him plus the major tranquilizer they had then put into his IV. The patient, who I will call Mr. Jones, was a fifty-something patient with

---

*This story originally appeared on Goulston's website and is used here by permission of the author.

AIDS (just after it was identified as an illness), with a terrible infection, who had been placed on a respirator. He had been pulling out his IVs and then pulling at his respirator and was in a state of what the surgeons called psychotic agitation.

When I entered Mr. Jones's room, he was lying with his arms and legs restrained. His eyes were as big as saucers and seemed to be screaming out to me. His eyes in fact grabbed hold of mine and I kept repeating, "What are you trying to tell me?" Because of the respirator, he couldn't speak. All he could do was groan in agony. I put a pen in his right hand close to the restraint on that wrist and put a piece of paper near it so he could write. All he could do was scribble something that didn't make any sense. I again repeated, "What is it?" And again he couldn't communicate what it was.

I concluded that what the surgeons had said was true and that Mr. Jones was psychotic and needing the restraints and the tranquilizer. I told him: "Mr. Jones, you have been pulling your IVs out and pulling at your respirator tubing, and we needed to restrain you and have also given you a tranquilizer to help you calm down. When you calm down, we will take you off the restraints. I will keep checking in to see how you are doing. Do you have any questions?" All Mr. Jones could do was stare at me with his eyes wide open in terror, which were now beginning to show the slightest signs of being tranquilized.

I checked in with him and with his surgeons over the next couple of days, but he was mostly sleeping.

Two days later I received a page from his attending chief surgical resident who in a rather curt manner said to me: "Hey, Mr. Jones is up, alert, off the respirator, and commanded us to call *you*. So I think you should come and see him as soon as you are able."

With trepidation, I went up to Mr. Jones's room. When I arrived, he was seated up in his bed and, in a nonpsychotic but very determined way, grabbed onto my eyes with his, said, "Please sit down," and with those eyes placed me in a chair.

His eyes never left mine, and I could not move mine away. Then in no uncertain terms and with an emphatic voice he said: "What I was trying to tell you was that a piece of the respirator tubing had broken off and was stuck in my throat. You do need to know that I will kill myself before I ever get into that situation again. Do you understand?"

My eyes winced and teared up as he revealed the answer to the mystery from my original visit. I wanted to look away but couldn't. Instead I said, "I'm so sorry that I didn't know that. And yes, I do understand that you will kill yourself before you have to go through something like that again."

And that is when I began to "listen into people's eyes." I just didn't know what to call it.

Our Mental Filters

The human brain filters information and quickly assigns labels for good reason: it's a basic and highly evolved survival function. Our mental filters help us assess threats and avoid danger.

Imagine you're in an unfamiliar city. It's late at night and you're walking back to your hotel when you consider taking a shortcut through a dark, empty, overgrown lot. But just as you start across the lot, you notice a couple of big guys in what look like hooded sweatshirts. They're watching you from the far side of the lot, waiting there. Do you still take the shortcut? How long does it take you to make the decision?

Chances are, sensing danger, you'd quickly turn around and head the other way. It's a situation where your mental filters kick in, not one where you need to gather more information and weigh the pros and cons. Our brains are designed to analyze situations and people in under one second, filtering information based on our knowledge and past experiences in order to assess threats, dangers, and risk. In this way, the brain's filtering process serves as an alarm system and "first responder."

The brain's filtering mechanism does an excellent job of keeping us alive and safe, but it's less helpful when it comes to listening. Let's say you're on a sales call, and the prospect is openly hostile to you. He refuses to shake your hand, keeping his arms crossed on his chest. "I don't trust salespeople," he says, scowling. "You're all liars."

Chances are, your brain will immediately label the guy a jerk, a grouch, someone you don't want to work with. And chances are, you'll write off the sale right then or, at the very least, have a much lower expectation of success. You might even return his hostility with your own.

But what if you learned that, prior to your meeting, the prospect had to take his mother to the hospital after she fell and broke her hip? Or what if you found out he'd hardly slept for three nights because his boss was breathing down his neck? Or that he got sold something that didn't work by the last two salespeople he dealt with?

Assigning labels based on initial impressions can prevent us from getting a person's whole story. In a dark, empty, overgrown lot, we don't need the whole story, but when tending relationships, we do. We can't prevent our brains from filtering, but we can be aware of and resist our instinct to quickly assign labels during selling situations.

Our Perfect Solutions

Imagine a seller who's worried about keeping his job. He's been under quota and under the gun for three quarters. Now he encounters a "suspect"—not yet even a prospect—who admits a big, juicy problem for which the embattled seller has the *perfect solution*. How long before the seller is fantasizing about this one deal changing his life? How long before he's calculating his commission check? How long before he stops actually listening to the buyer and interrupts to say, "We've solved your problem dozens of times. What *you need* is our *xyz* solution."

The excitement of a perfect match can cause sellers to "prematurely elaborate." They stop listening and go to their solutions too early, putting too much pressure on the buyer and inadvertently causing tension. The more excitement for the solution, the less they listen.

It's ironic, of course. The seller's genuine enthusiasm to rescue the buyer prevents the seller from getting the buyer to really open up. And in many cases, the seller will be right. But *being right* is itself a listening block, putting the buyer and seller in opposition: if someone is right, then someone else must be wrong.

Mike's Story: Premature Elaboration

During the SPIN project at Xerox Corporation, we charted the positive behaviors of our top sellers. We made a surprising observation. Neil Rackham, the project lead, presented his findings to our executives. On an easel, he drew a graph in which the y axis represented sales performance and the x axis represented time. Neil then drew a curve that started low and rose steadily over time, peaking at 18 months and then dropping sharply. He informed the executives that this line represented the group sales performance of Xerox sellers hired straight out of college over their first 18 months with the company.

"You can almost set your watch by it," he said.

Why were Xerox salespeople crashing and burning at 18 months? Today, when we open this question up to participants in the workshop, we hear a lot of possible reasons: maybe Xerox cut the salespeople's territory, maybe the salespeople were getting fewer leads from marketing, maybe the salespeople tended to get new managers or new sales plans after 18 months, and so on.

Neil arrived at an altogether different and less obvious conclusion. As he saw it, the real reason was behavioral. Over their first several months with Xerox, newly hired salespeople had the opportunity to learn every combination of Xerox product applicability to a range of problems. Neil theorized that salespeople mastered this information—that they became "expert" salespeople—at about 18 months.

At that point, a Xerox salesperson was able to anticipate a prospect's problem based on very little information. As soon as the prospect got the first few words out of her mouth, the salesperson would stop listening and respond with some version of "I know exactly why you are having this problem and how we can solve it with our product *xyz*." The seller would generally be correct, accurately assessing the problem, offering exactly what the prospect needed . . . and then the seller would lose the sale.

So why was this happening? Premature elaboration. The salespeople's behavior was off-putting, causing buyers to resist instead of receive. The sellers demonstrated a combination of classic listening blocks: impatience, mind reading, being right, advising, knowing all the answers, and so on. They were doing everything except actually listening. They were telling buyers what the buyers needed before they had earned the right, before they'd built any trust.

It's a mistake endemic to people who are selling as "experts"—solution sellers, sellers helping their customers solve problems with their products. As Neil put it, "When you're selling, your expertise becomes your enemy." Your expertise may make you "right," but your buyer still needs time to move through his or her buy cycle, processing information along the way. It's like when Dr. Phil asks, "Would you rather be *right*, or would you rather be in a relationship?"

Neil's explanation also accounts for why Xerox salespeople tended to do better *before* they became experts. A seller in his third or fourth month with the company wasn't yet able to fully anticipate a prospect's needs based on cursory information. He had no clue if he could help the buyer. So instead of interrupting the buyer and telling him what the problem was and how he was going to solve it, the seller was inclined, out of necessity, to demonstrate sincere curiosity about the buyer's problem. Instead of saying, "I have exactly the product to meet your needs," the inexperienced seller was more likely to say, "I'm not sure if I can help you or not. Let me summarize what I know so far." In this way, the seller received validation from the buyer that he "got" the buyer's problem. Instead of cramming a solution down the buyer's throat, the seller might then say, "I'm going to share your situation with our experts at the office and get back to you."

And so the sellers *without* expertise made better sales calls than the impatient experts.

Quotas

Even in the go-go business climate of the 1990s, fewer than 50 percent of salespeople in the B2B information technology market made their quotas. It's even worse today—much worse. If quotas are the benchmark, the vast majority of salespeople are failing at their jobs every year.

The result? They're in a constant state of worry, feeling perpetually pressured and behind. By necessity, they go into sales calls with a clear agenda: "How can I get this person to share his pain so I can sell him something to cure it?" It's a mind-set that isn't at all conducive to listening.

A big part of the problem is the quota system itself, which, in a misguided attempt to "motivate" sellers, is often rigged against them. Based on our research with client sales managers, there simply aren't enough opportunities in most businesses' pipelines for all their salespeople to have a realistic shot at making their quotas. In fact, only about 17 percent of sellers are likely to do so.

Traditional Sales Tools

We all know the playbooks: question-based selling, SPIN, 9 Boxes, Solution Prompters, diagnostic questions. The list of consultative-based selling models goes on and on. But after more than three decades of such models, nothing much has changed in the sales industry.

We now believe the lack of emphasis placed on listening is a big reason these models failed. The initial research established that the most successful sellers were asking buyers specific questions, so we developed selling models based on questions: diagnose and prescribe. In our old sales-training workshops, we used to teach sellers to ask a sequence of questions in a particular order. The goal was to diagnose the buyer's problem with a bias toward the seller's product or solution.

In retrospect, it's clear why these models weren't effective for most sellers. For starters, look up *question* in a thesaurus. You'll see synonyms such as *debate, conflict, controversy, doubt, examination, inquisition, interrogation, wringer, argument, challenge, dispute, objection,* and *protest*—not words that characterize collaborative two-way *communication*. Questions have become formulaic.

Furthermore, all of the models more or less resembled the Socratic method, named after the Greek philosopher Socrates, in which the basic form is "a series of questions formulated as tests of logic and fact intended to debate another person." As Wikipedia.com defines it:

> The Socratic method . . . is a form of inquiry and debate between *individuals* with opposing viewpoints *[emphasis added]* based on asking and answering questions to stimulate critical thinking and to illuminate ideas. It is a dialectical method, often involving an oppositional discussion in which the defense of one point of view is pitted against the defense of another. . . . *The Socratic method is a* negative method of hypothesis elimination, *in that better hypotheses are found by steadily identifying and eliminating those that lead to* contradictions.

Socratic questioning is often used by attorneys to get a witness to reveal a piece of information in court. The problem is that buyers should not be "tested" like witnesses on the witness stand.

The traditional models were based on the available research of the day and had the right intention—to get buyers to open up. But they were going about it all wrong, posing questions in a way guaranteed to trigger a buyer's left-brain barriers, skepticism, and defense mechanisms. Buyers didn't cooperate with prescriptive questioning models because, as with Socratic questioning, they put the two parties—seller and buyer—in competition with one another.

Dr. Daniel Siegel describes the interrogate-judge-fix model as a "pathway to disconnection." The pathway to collaborative communication, by contrast, involves a very different model: explore-understand-join.

The problem with traditional models wasn't the questions; it was how they were being used. In training sellers to ask a sequence of questions—a script, essentially—we were inadvertently encouraging them to already be thinking about the next question while the buyer was still answering the last one. That is, we were training them *not* to listen.

As the French author François de La Rochefoucauld once put it, "The reason why so few people are agreeable in conversation is that each is thinking more about what he intends to say than about what others are saying, and we never listen when we are eager to speak."

Today, we have a different understanding of the relationship between listening and questioning: listening is not part of questioning; questioning is part of listening. We now understand that questions should be used with sincere curiosity, to sincerely understand the buyer's story. They can't be scripted ahead of time. Our questions should be about *what we hear* from our buyers.

Type A Personality

As a profession, sales tends to attract "Type A" personalities, people who are ambitious, aggressive, controlling, highly competitive, impatient, time-conscious, hard driving, and tightly wound. Salespeople with Type A personalities are often workaholics who multitask, push themselves with deadlines, and have no tolerance for delays and ambiguity. They tend to have an answer for everything. Above all, they always have an eye on the finish line and are in a hurry to get there.

Now picture yourself as a customer on a car lot, in a retail store, or in a B2B sales meeting. Would you want to open up and reveal yourself to someone like this? If you have a Type A personality yourself, perhaps such a seller would have a chance with you, but otherwise, it's a recipe for failure, particularly when a Type A seller meets up with an introverted Type B buyer.

As sellers, we must be aware of our Type A tendencies and try to rein them in—try to be patient, relaxed, easygoing, and nurturing. Otherwise, our personalities will prevent us from doing the kind of listening that leads to real emotional connections and, ultimately, to successful selling.

Empathic Listening

While we can't realistically hope to eliminate all of our listening blocks, just being aware of them opens us up to a world of real, empathic listening. We listen empathically not only to get information from buyers but also to connect with them and get them to open up to us, which is the first step toward moving away from resistance and allowing oneself to be influenced and agreeable to new ideas.

Instead of listening with the intent to find a "pain" or problem that we can address, we must listen with *the intent to understand*. This is empathic listening—engaging people in order to understand their ideas and feelings, their point of view, where they're coming from. This is how we get someone's whole story.

During a sales call, a buyer sizes up a seller, imagining what it would be like to work with that person: *Who is this person? Is she only out for her own good, or does she have my interests in mind as well? Does she "get" me?* If a buyer feels that a seller is trying to persuade him—that is, to push an agenda—the buyer will instinctively resist. By contrast, if a buyer feels cared about and tended to by the seller, the buyer will instinctively move toward cooperation.

The psychoanalyst Wilfred Bion says, "The purest form of listening is to listen without memory or desire." When we listen with memory, we push an old agenda. When we listen with desire, we push a new agenda. When we listen without memory or desire, we let go of our agendas in a way that allows buyers to open up.

Dr. Edwin Shneidman, the noted suicidologist and thanatologist, makes a similar point: "When you listen for the pain, hurt, and fear in people, it is always there. And when people sense you doing that with no other motive than to alleviate all of those, they will lower their walls and reveal them to you."

To listen without an agenda is hard, of course, because on some level, we always have one—to succeed at our jobs as salespeople. Ironically, we are most likely to advance our agendas during a sales call when we forget about them and focus on understanding the buyer instead.

Empathic listening involves much more than just hearing a buyer's words. As we showed in Figure 7.1, the majority of human communication (93 percent) involves things other than spoken words (7 percent). To listen empathically, we need to be in tune with a buyer's body language, because that's how the buyer will primarily communicate his feelings and truest intentions. Are the buyer's words in harmony with his tone of voice and nonverbal cues? Is the buyer trying to tell you something that he isn't actually saying? Is the buyer telling you something that he doesn't mean to reveal? Recall that our fastest and most evolved cognitive transmissions are from mind to body, not mind to mouth. Words can be misleading, but the body doesn't lie. At the same time, body language doesn't always give us the full story. If a buyer's arms are crossed, he may be feeling guarded; then again, he may just be cold. To get a buyer's full story, we must synthesize what we're hearing and seeing and use whole-brain listening—emotional receptivity plus cognitive analysis. Whole-brain listening involves:

- **What are we listening to?** What is said, how it's said, what's not said.
- **What are we listening with?** Our ears and eyes, as well as our heads and hearts.

Any questions we ask a buyer should come not from a sales script but from what we learn through empathic listening; they should pertain not to a sales agenda but to a sincere curiosity about where the buyer is coming from. If we pay attention to the clues a buyer gives us, they will lead us to a deeper understanding of that person and his or her needs.

Ben's Story: Follow the Bread Crumbs

Shortly after reading Dr. Mark Goulston's story about listening into people's eyes, I had the good fortune of meeting Dr. Daniel Siegel and listening to him speak to a group of parents at a conference in Los Angeles. In his bestselling book, *Parenting from the Inside Out,* Siegel discusses how to achieve a deeper level of understanding your children by learning to focus on more than just the surface level of their behavior.

That same night, I got a firsthand lesson from my daughter, Zoe, in how misleading the "surface level" can be. After my wife and I left Dr. Siegel's talk, we took our two girls to the mall. As we were passing the store Forever 21, Zoe, who was 10 years old at the time, said she wanted to go in because there was a pair of pants she wanted.

"How much?" I said.

"Seventy dollars."

"No way," I said.

She turned to her mom and started negotiating with her instead. Recognizing that I was now irrelevant to the conversation, I said I'd meet them in front of the store in 20 minutes and went for a walk. When I got back 20 minutes later, Zoe had not one but two pairs of pants.

Fast-forward to three-thirty the following afternoon. I was working from my home office when I heard my wife and Zoe having an argument. It sounded more heated than usual, so I went into Zoe's room to see what was going on. She was yelling at her mom.

"Why did you make me wear these pants?" she said. "I hate you. I hate these pants."

I couldn't believe what I was hearing. "Zoe," I said, "what are you talking about? No one made you wear these pants. You *begged* us to buy them."

"No, I didn't," she said. "I hate you guys. You made me wear them." At which point she took off the pants and threw them against the wall.

That did it. We really lit into her, calling her spoiled and ungrateful, reminding her again that she was the one who'd wanted the pants in the first place. Zoe was shouting back at us the whole time. Finally my wife had had enough. She stormed out of the room and slammed the door. I did the same, going the other way and slamming Zoe's other door, and went back to my office, steaming. Zoe was still yelling at us from her room.

The first thing I saw when I got back to my office was Siegel's book, *Parenting from the Inside Out*, right there on my desk. I was trying to calm down. "Okay," I thought. "What was it Siegel said during his talk?"

He'd said that our children will tell us their stories, but not necessarily with their words. He encouraged us to "scratch beneath the surface" and listen with our hearts. He talked about being aware, looking for clues—often visual clues. I likened the idea of clues to the bread crumbs in the fairy tale *Hansel and Gretel*. "Follow the bread crumbs and they'll lead you home."

So I asked myself, could the pants alone really be the cause of so much hostility? Of course not. I started going over the visual clues from our argument, looking for a bread crumb. Then I took a deep breath, headed back to Zoe's room, and knocked on her door.

"What do you want?" she yelled.

"Just to listen." I came in and sat on her bed. "Zoe," I said. "I noticed you threw your pants against the wall."

She was still worked up. She ignored me and starting pulling papers from her backpack, crumpling them and throwing them into the trashcan.

"Did you have a test today?" I said, grasping for another clue.

"I hate school," she said.

"Sounds like you had a frustrating day."

"Frustrating?" She looked at me like I was an idiot.

"Worse than frustrating?" I said.

She stared down at the ball of crumpled paper in her fist. The anger drained out of her. Her eyes welled up.

"What happened?" I said.

That's when she told me her story. In the cafeteria that day, she'd taken her lunch over to a table where her friends Jennifer and Sara were sitting.

"But when I sat down, Jennifer wouldn't even look at me," she said, barely able to get the words out. "She just turned to Sara and said, 'Let's sit at another table.' Then they got up and moved."

Seeing her so brokenhearted, my eyes welled up too. I felt so helpless.

"Come here," I said, making room on the bed. She sat down and I put my arm around her shoulder. "I'm sorry, honey," I said. "Kids can be so cruel. That totally sucks. I love you so much." I didn't know what else to say or do, so I just held her.

And then a surprising thing happened. Once Zoe calmed down, she got up, picked her pants up off the floor, and folded them neatly. Then she went into the kitchen where her mom was. I couldn't hear what they said to each other, but I saw them embrace.

Back in my office, I remember feeling so relieved that she'd opened up to me, and it was all because I'd scratched beneath the surface and followed the bread crumbs. How lucky I was. If this would have happened only 24 hours earlier, before I had listened to Dr. Siegel's talk, I would have never scratched beneath the surface and would have written her off as acting like a brat.

Feeling Felt and the Mirror Neuron Receptor Deficit

Before a buyer will allow herself to be influenced—before she will open up to a seller and begin the "buy-in" cycle— she must first "feel felt." Empathic listening is the key to making someone feel felt.

In his book *Just Listen: Discover the Secret to Getting Through to Absolutely Anyone,* Dr. Mark Goulston describes what happens when someone doesn't feel felt. He calls it the "mirror neuron receptor deficit (MNRD)." As discussed in Chapter 2, mirror neurons are brain cells that fire both when we act and when we observe the same action performed by another person. They essentially "mirror" the behavior of the other person, as though we ourselves were acting. When we watch another person laugh, for instance, the same neurons fire in our brain as when we ourselves laugh.

Neuroscientists have discovered that when a caregiver "tends" a child and makes that child feel felt, neurons are stimulated in the child, and the development of neuron mirroring occurs. Moreover, the circuitry of the brain is altered in such a way that new ideas can be formed with greater clarity. Conversely, when a caregiver is unresponsive or confusing, or when he or she lacks attunement with a child, that child experiences an unsettled emotional state.

Mirror neurons are a big part of what make emotions contagious. We have a biological need to be mirrored. When our feelings are mirrored, we feel felt, and we reciprocate, instinctively trying to satisfy the other person's emotional needs. When our feelings aren't mirrored—when we experience MNRD—we feel underwhelmed and unsatisfied, and may even subconsciously act out, attempting to provoke in others the emotions we're feeling. More often, though, we just clam up.

Ben's Story: Talking to a Machine

When Mike and I decided to write this book, I had no idea where to start. I'd never done much writing. I didn't consider myself a writer. I certainly didn't enjoy writing. So how was I supposed to get everything in my head down on paper?

I tried everything I could think of. I locked myself in my office for hours at a time. I gave myself deadlines and ultimatums. I recorded and transcribed my workshops. Nothing worked.

Finally, a friend suggested I try transcription dictation software. All I'd have to do was talk into the computer, and the software would do the rest, transcribing my speech into written words. It seemed like a great idea. After all, as a workshop leader, I talk for a living. I could do what I do best, orally sharing my stories, and they would magically appear onscreen. Why should I kill myself trying to write a book when I could talk one instead?

I purchased the most expensive dictation software I could find, downloaded it, bought a good microphone, and began talking into the computer. I was excited and confident. I had hopes of cranking out the book in a matter of weeks.

But it wasn't as easy as I'd imagined. I found myself starting and stopping every two seconds. I couldn't get a whole story out, not even a little three-minute story I'd told scores of times. I was too self-conscious. Everything I said sounded contrived and robotic.

After a week or so, I just gave up. In fact, I was starting to worry I'd somehow lost the ability to communicate my stories at all. But of course I hadn't. As soon as I was back in the workshop, telling stories to real people who mirrored my feelings and emoted with me, the stories flowed just like they always had.

The whole experience made me all the more aware of the reciprocal, collaborative nature of conversation and story-telling. Without a human being there to listen empathically and tend my story, talking to a machine had made *me* sound like a machine, too.

People really do want to tell their stories. It's just hard to get them out if we don't have empathic listeners. And talking to a bad listener—someone who just wants the facts, someone who is emotionless, someone with an *agenda*—isn't much better than talking to a computer.

Listening Model

Listening empathically is difficult, but it's an invaluable skill, both in professional and private life. What makes an empathic listener? Consider the Chinese character for listening—it tells us a lot about what listening really is (see Figure 8.1).

The first thing to note is that the symbol comprises much more than just hearing words (ear). Listening also involves the eyes, the heart, and undivided attention. The last feature of the symbol—king—connotes the idea that when truly listening to someone, we treat that person like royalty.

To embody such a comprehensive model of listening, a listener must demonstrate three qualities:

o Awareness
o Encouragement
o Reflection

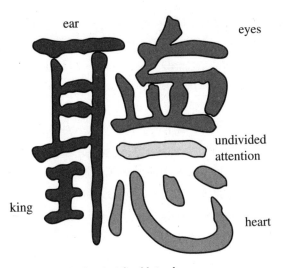

ear

eyes

undivided
attention

king

heart

Figure 8.1 The Chinese Symbol for Listening

Awareness

Empathic listening requires an awareness of a buyer's non-verbal cues. Traditional consultative question-based sales models (the scripted lists of questions from the playbook) involve left-brain thinking, listening with your ears. By contrast, awareness requires right-brain thinking, listening with your ears, eyes, and heart.

In order to tune in to buyers, we must stop thinking about the next question we're going to ask and be fully "present" in order to absorb what they're communicating to us, both verbally and nonverbally.

A buyer with his chin down may be feeling skeptical. A buyer with his chin out may be defensive or even defiant. A nod from the neck up often connotes reserved agreement—you're not in yet, but you've got a foot in the door. A truly relaxed nod through the neck and shoulders tells you that the buyer is "with" you.

Is a buyer saying what he really thinks and feels? If he touches his face, that's a cue that he might be withholding something. Children instinctively cover their mouths before they lie. As adults, we've learned not to do that, so our brains curb the impulse and send our hands elsewhere—sometimes a scratch of the head or nose. Most nonverbal cues you will understand intuitively. The key is being fully present so that you're aware of the cues in the first place.

Awareness is particularly challenging when you're on the phone and can't see your buyer's body language. All you have to go on is what you can hear—words, tone of voice, speech rhythms (e.g., hesitations), and so forth. But with experience, it can be done. We actually role-play phone calls in our workshops by having participants sit back-to-back. During these exercises, the listener guesses the speaker's body language gestures and facial expressions, writing them down. Participants who are focused on being aware typically guess correctly.

Ben's Story: Meeting Senator Obama

In 2006, I made a business trip to Chicago, taking the last flight of the day from LAX to O'Hare. The plane arrived at midnight. By then, the baggage area was almost deserted, but the luggage from our flight was delayed. I was just standing there, killing time, when I recognized a familiar face on the other side of the carousel. It was the senator from Illinois, Barack Obama, with his wife, Michelle—no entourage, just the two of them sitting there waiting for their suitcases.

Obama wouldn't announce his candidacy for president until a few months later, in 2007, but he was already expected to run for office. Just a couple of weeks earlier, I'd heard him on the radio and remembered sharing his frustration that the Democratic Party wasn't able to tell its story as clearly as the Republicans told theirs. "We don't have a clear narrative that the American public is buying," he'd said. "The Republicans do."

Standing there at baggage claim, I wanted to meet him, but I didn't have the nerve. *Go on*, I told myself. *What do you have to lose? And when are you going to get another chance to meet a possible future president of the United States?*

I had one of our old books, *CustomerCentric Selling*, in my briefcase. I pulled it out, worked up my courage, and walked over to Obama. I was so nervous, I don't remember exactly what I said, but it was something along the lines of, "Mr. Senator, I'm sorry to bother you. I'm sure you're exhausted, but I just heard an interview where you talked about your frustration that our party can't seem to tell its story clearly. I'm in the business of helping companies tell their stories, and I thought you might be interested in our book."

Actually, I doubt I was that coherent. As I held out the book, I hoped he didn't notice my hand shaking. The only other time I'd been that nervous was when I'd met Magic Johnson when I was 14.

"Thank you," Obama said, taking the book. "That is so kind of you." Then he handed the book back to me, pulled a pen from his coat pocket, and said, "Will you sign this for me?"

I took the pen, but I didn't know if I'd be able to write anything legible. I'm sure I must have seemed like a freak. Obama wasn't put off, though. Instead, much to my surprise, he calmly began telling me how to spell his name.

"It's B – A – R – A – C – K," he said.

I knew what he was doing—he'd sensed how nervous I was, so he was trying to put me at ease, give me a moment to collect myself. And it worked. When I was done inscribing the book, I handed it back to him, and we struck up a conversation.

"Are you coming in from L.A.?" he said.

It turns out we were on the same flight. I asked him what he'd been doing in Los Angeles, and we ended up chatting for about 15 minutes, until the luggage arrived.

The point of the story is *not* that Obama read our book, ran for president, and got elected because of that fateful midnight meeting at O'Hare. The point is that he was attuned to my nonverbal cues—that he "listened" with more than just his ears—and was therefore able to calm me. If he'd been a salesperson, I'd have been happy to buy anything he was selling.

Encouragement

When we encourage someone in conversation, we help that person feel that it's safe to reveal whatever it is she wants to say. Often this encouragement involves questions, but for a question to be encouraging, it must not make the speaker feel like she's on the witness stand. Encouraging questions are based on what we're learning, in real time, through empathic listening.

Recall Dr. Daniel Siegel's advice: "Scratch beneath the surface." Follow the bread crumbs and they'll lead you home. When a person communicates something to us, spoken or unspoken, we can use that piece of information, a bread crumb, to encourage them to communicate more to us. A scratch of the head, a shift in tone of voice, a change in eye contact—they're all bread crumbs.

Encouragement can be verbal or nonverbal. Nonverbal "questions"—questions you ask not with words but with facial expressions and body language—include the following:

- o *"Hmm."* We say this with our bodies when we nod along to what a speaker is saying and express attentiveness and focus through our facial expressions. Steady eye contact also lets a speaker know that you're focused on what he's saying, fully present.
- o *"Tell me more."* Leaning in toward a speaker expresses strong engagement with what is being said.
- o *Pauses.* People tend to fill a pause by talking. Coupled with relaxed body language, a pause creates an opening in conversation for the speaker to continue a train of thought or start a new one. Too often in conversation, we jump in and cut other people off before they've finished what they have to say. Pauses convey to a speaker that you are processing what they are saying and that their thoughts and feelings are important to you.

Likewise, verbal questions can also communicate interest and engagement, and help your buyers keep going until they've told their whole stories. The shorter the question, the more natural it feels. The longer the question, the more rehearsed and proscribed it feels. Try to keep your questions brief, such as:

- o *"Then what?"* This is the most basic question to keep a narrative moving forward, conveying a desire to know what happens next. "Tell me more about . . ." works, too.
- o *"Why?"* On the surface, this question asks the speaker to clarify something, but it's also a great way to nudge a speaker to more fully develop a part of his or her story.
- o *"I don't get what you meant by xyz. Can you help me understand it better?"* (Or, *"Can you go back to that?"*). This is a more direct way to ask for clarification.

Having your story tended—having a listener attuned to your emotions and encouraging you—can be unsettling if you're not used to it, especially (1) in a business setting; (2) if, like many of us, you lack a real language of emotion; and (3) if the listener starts asking you pointed questions about how you *feel*.

A subtle yet effective way to encourage a speaker to share more, especially feelings, is with sincere questions that seek to clarify your understanding or your own feeling. "Nonquestions" provide a less off-putting way of encouraging a speaker to talk about her or his feelings. A nonquestion is an implied question—a remark or observation not framed as an interrogative (i.e., not using a question mark) that still provides the speaker a chance to "answer." This is an approach to encourage a speaker to share his or her feelings using both nonquestions and clarifying questions. Try using these in the order they appear:

o *"It sounds like you were feeling _____ [name an emotion]. Is that correct, or is it something else?"* Give the speaker the authority to name his or her emotion.
o *"Could you tell me how much you're feeling _____ [restate that emotion]?"* Give the speaker an opportunity to indicate the degree of feeling.
o *"And, why is it that you're feeling that way? If it's okay with you, I'd like to know where that is coming from."* Give the speaker a chance to clarify or elaborate. Help the speaker acknowledge why he or she feels that way. That person will appreciate that you care enough to explore the source of those feelings with him or her.

Reflection

How do you know whether you've really gotten a buyer's whole story? How does the buyer know if you "get" him?

Once you've tended a buyer's story by being aware and offering encouragement, it's necessary to demonstrate reflection, to synthesize everything the buyer has communicated to you, both verbally and nonverbally, and reflect it back by paraphrasing it. A person will be grateful to have his story reflected back for two reasons: (1) to make sure you really understand what he's trying to convey, and (2) to let *him* know you "get" him. Here's what you can reflect it back with:

o "Let me put this all together. It sounded like you said . . ."
o "Let me see if I got you right. You said . . ."

As you paraphrase the buyer's story, make sure you reflect not just the facts of what happened but also the emotions involved—coherence plus context. In doing so, you'll be helping your buyer think in story, helping him make his information "storiable."

At the conclusion of your reflection, how can you know that you truly "get" the person? Consider what is unconsciously on the mind of a speaker:

o "Does she get it?" = Implies situational awareness
o "Does she get us?" = Implies company awareness
o "Does she get me?" = Implies personal awareness

Personal awareness can have a much greater impact on a meeting than situational or company awareness. A powerful question to confirm that you get the other person is to end your reflection this way:

○ "Do I get *you?*"

When a buyer hears his story from someone else, has it played back to him, and is then asked, "Do I get you?" it can have a profound impact: *Wow, this person really gets* me. The buyer will feel further validated if you're able to articulate how you personally connected with the story:

○ "That makes sense to me because . . ."
○ "I think I understand how you feel because . . ."
○ "I felt _____ [name an emotion] when you told me the part about . . ."
○ "I imagine you must have felt _____ [name an emotion] . . ."

In his book *Mindsight,* Dr. Daniel Siegel discusses the importance of attunement and reflection in the relationship between parent and child. A child's ability to experience meaningful connection is shaped at an early age by a parent's level of attunement. When a parent can reflect back to a child what the child is experiencing, the child will have greater clarity about how he feels. Empathic listening and reflection similarly allow you to help a buyer have greater clarity about his own feelings and stories—past, present, and future. Once you've listened empathically to a buyer's story, demonstrating awareness, encouragement, and reflection, you're ready for a new story as you continue up the rungs of the ladder toward the resolution of the buyer's story in which the buyer is influenced to believe what you believe and take a chance on you.

But What About the Buyer's Challenges?

After we talk about empathic listening in the workshop, a lot of participants still have the same concern. "I get why stories are important," they tell us. "I get the listening model. But what about the buyer's challenges, pains, and issues? Don't I need to ask about those, too?"

The answer, of course, is right there in the question. When you "get" a buyer's whole story, you're guaranteed to get all of his challenges, plus a lot more:

1. You'll circumvent the buyer's instinctive left-brain resistance to persuasion and change.
2. You'll establish an emotional connection and get the buyer to open up, the first step in influencing someone to believe what you believe.
3. You'll likely get stuff you didn't even know you needed, contextual information that will inform both your relationship with the buyer and your understanding of how to proceed up the story ladder.

From a buyer's perspective, having the torch passed to you so you can tell your story feels very different from being asked to "share your pains." Let's face it. Buyers don't view salespeople as doctors: "Thanks for coming to see me, Ms. Salesperson. Let me tell you about my pains!" On the contrary, buyers view salespeople as . . . salespeople. They're people who want to sell them something—people with agendas. And buyers are very familiar with other salespeople who've already tried to "diagnose their problem."

By approaching buyers through story and then passing the torch, you'll distinguish yourself from all those other salespeople and gain a fuller understanding of your buyers, including but not limited to their challenges, which will come to you in the form of complications in the arc of their stories. Remember, the brain responds positively in story mode, whether you're listening to a story or being given the opportunity to tell one.

The ultimate goal is to use your storytelling and story-tending skills to move buyers up the ladder, helping them build their own stories along the way. The only part of their story they won't yet be able to share is the resolution—the future time in which their problems have been addressed. Your goal is to help them build a vision of that future that includes *you*.

Ben's Story: Getting the Whole Story

In 2010, I had a sales call on the phone with an IBM executive. It was a big opportunity for Story Leaders. Mike and I were hoping IBM would make our workshops an important part of their sales training.

The prospect, Gary, started by giving me *his* point of view on sales enablement, sales training, and what sales effectiveness meant to him. His definition of selling was completely different from mine, and from the way he was describing his beliefs, I began to think he was someone I could never sell to, someone who would never be an ally of ours within the corporation. Also, the way he was addressing me sounded almost confrontational; the more he talked, the more defensive I became. *This guy just doesn't get it,* I thought.

That's when I started to get anxious, which in turn made me want to cut to the chase, rush to the finish line, and get the sales call over and done with. I lost sight of caring about him as a person; all I cared about was his business.

In other words, I basically forgot everything that's in this book.

Fortunately, Gary is a very extroverted guy, and he ended up talking for so long that I had time to cool down. I happened to glance up at the bulletin board next to my computer and saw the words *story tending* posted there. I recalled the things I teach in the workshop. *Do it,* I told myself. *Tend to his story.*

When Gary finally finished making his points, he turned the floor over to me. "So how can Story Leaders help?" he said.

Instead of diving into how I could solve his problem— as I'd been tempted to do only moments earlier—I said, "I think we might be able to help, Gary, but I also think I'd understand where you're coming from better if you told me your whole story."

The invitation to tell a story can be just as powerful as the offer of hearing one, and sure enough, Gary launched right in. "Sure," he said. "Let me go back. I started at IBM 24 years ago. I was actually an intern in college, got an opportunity to go into sales, and took my lumps . . ." He talked for several more minutes as I focused on staying tuned in and encouraging him with an occasional question about what I was hearing. The amazing thing was, when Gary got the chance to share his whole story, he told me so much more than he had during his lecture at the beginning of our call. By the time he was done, not only had he detailed the challenges he was facing with his sales force, but he also let down his guard and revealed some things he'd been holding back earlier.

"Actually, Ben," he said, "our people hardly ever get customers to share their real pains. A very small percentage. I do have one rep who really gets customers to open up.

If you talked to her, you'd think she's more of a storyteller than a salesperson. . . ." And so his story kept building, with more color, more frankness, and more emotion.

When he was done, I didn't start telling Gary about Story Leaders, and he didn't ask again. Instead, he asked about me: "How about you, Ben? What's your story?"

By the end of the conversation, I had no doubt that we "got" each other, that our mirror neurons were doing their job, that we'd established an emotional connection. I'd also gotten everything I needed to know to make the sale, and I'd done it by forgetting about my agenda altogether and focusing instead on listening and tending to Gary's story.

CHAPTER 9

Shifting the Herd:
The Enterprise Sale

> Change does not happen from the top down, it happens from the bottom up.
>
> —Barack Obama

How Enterprises Change

In Chapter 5, we explored why it's so difficult to influence people to change: change is slow, and it requires struggle. Influencing enterprises to change is even more daunting. Instead of trying to overcome a single person's natural resistance to try a new way, we're challenging the status quo of a large organization made up of an untold number of individuals, in a variety of silos, most of whom we don't even have direct access to.

In *Solution Selling* and *CustomerCentric Selling*, we taught sellers "California selling": "Call high, stay high." A key element of our qualification model was "getting access to a power sponsor" or "decision-making-level" person, someone within an organization who has "budget," the means and authority to spend. We believed that in order to sell big to an enterprise, the seller needed to get in near the top. Since then, we've learned there is a lot more to it.

Mike's Story: Keith's One Guy (Part One)

Back in my Solution Selling and CustomerCentric Selling days, I had dozens of affiliates selling my sales methodology. Of those, one affiliate brought in more revenue than all the others combined.

Keith was the very best at both selling and teaching our methodology. At the time, I didn't really get why he was so much better than everyone else in our organization at selling to large enterprises. Looking back, of course, I recognize that he was a masterful storyteller and story tender, but there was something else in his approach to the enterprise sales cycle that set him apart.

This was the early 1990s. Solution Selling was starting to take off, but mostly with small-to-medium-sized businesses. With release of my book *Solution Selling* in 1993, I was able to call into larger enterprises. One day, I got the contact number for IBM's president of North American operations, and I cold-called him. It began as a promising call; I got him on the line and we had a conversation. However, I was quickly relegated to the black hole of the IBM training department. I'd done exactly what I taught—called high, to the C suite—but my conversation with the prospect had nevertheless led down a rabbit hole to nowhere.

A year later, I got a call from Keith explaining that he had an "in" with a small IBM business unit. His champion was a midlevel sales director who wanted us to do a workshop for his group. At the time, the status quo at IBM amounted to little more than sales training by subject: negotiation, proposal writing, presentation skills, handling objections, and so on. This one sales director believed Solution Selling represented a new way.

I was skeptical that this one person, this one workshop, would turn into a larger opportunity. I remembered asking Keith, "Do you have access to power?" Keith told me no, but he felt comfortable expending his efforts on this midlevel sales director. In my cold call the year before, I'd gotten to the executive who ran all of North America for IBM, several levels higher than the one Keith had access to, and it had gotten us nowhere. Of course, I gave Keith the green light, but I didn't have much faith that it would go beyond a single departmental workshop; Keith's "in" was simply too low.

Boy, was I wrong! After that first workshop, Keith's one guy not only introduced Keith to every one of his peers but he also sold for him. And the attendees of the workshop told their peers about Solution Selling, who then told their peers. A movement of believers coalesced, and those believers became internal sellers for Keith, almost as if they were the sales reps and Keith were the sales manager. Within three months, his single workshop with his "one guy" had turned into a half-dozen workshops.

Why did Solution Selling take off at IBM? At the time, the company didn't have a formal, structured sales process, and those managers and reps who were exposed to Solution Selling saw it as a new way, a departure from the status quo. The groups that went through our workshops became "tribes" that then spread to message to other tribes, eventually forming a virtual movement within the organization that multiplied exponentially. Before long, I was getting bigger and bigger royalty checks from Keith.

Tribes

In his book *Tribes: We Need You to Lead Us*, bestselling author Seth Godin defines a tribe as any group of people, large or small, who are connected to one another, a leader, and an idea. As human social units, tribes are naturally occurring groups. We're all members of tribes—both in our personal lives and at work. We form tribes inside of companies. It's what we do; it's what we've always done.

"Each tribe has a tribal leader," writes Godin, "connecting people with ideas."

Tribal leaders find others who share their belief, or they influence others to believe what they believe or value. Tribal leaders assemble tribes that assemble other tribes. That's how an idea can become a movement.

It's a phenomenon familiar to sociologists and anthropologists. Researchers have studied large herds of animals to better understand how change happens in the wild. The conventional wisdom had always held that pack leaders were responsible for a herd's shifts and direction changes. Researchers have repeatedly observed that this is not the case. Herd movement turns out to be less top-down—more democratic—than people previously believed. Any single animal within a herd can start a shift in the herd's direction. All it takes is one animal who senses a need, such as the threat of a predator, and moves away from it. Then a few others follow, forming a subgroup (a tribe). Then other subgroups form and make the move, until the subgroups make up 51 percent of the herd. Fifty-one percent is the tipping point at which the whole herd then moves together.

In observing this phenomenon, researchers have proven that it's not necessarily pack leaders who influence change; it can be any one animal within the herd. In fact, the pack leader is among the least likely to influence change, because the pack leader is generally buffered and surrounded, insulated in such a way that he can't sense the need for change. If the herd were to rely only on the pack leader, it would fail to make necessary moves and changes.

Such was the case with IBM. From his insulated position high up within the enterprise, the senior executive I originally spoke with didn't see a need for change. It wasn't until Keith succeeded in influencing a tribal leader who then went on to influence other tribes that our message spread and eventually worked its way up. Once that happened, it was little surprise that Solution Selling met with favor at the C level. Senior executives love consensus, and a grassroots movement of tribes fits the bill.

Modern psychological and economic researchers have observed that humans naturally prefer democracy (e.g., 51 percent rules) as opposed to top-down leadership or government by the few (e.g., oligarchy). As members of subgroups (tribes) that make up larger groups (herds), we are all wired to move with the herd.

Herd behavior accounts for how humans in a group can act together organically, without planned direction. Mirror neurons—triggering our natural inclination to reflect the emotions of others—facilitate this process. Herd behavior can be observed during stock market bubbles and crashes and street demonstrations; at sporting events and religious gatherings; during episodes of mob violence;

and even in everyday decision making, judgment, and opinion forming.

Consider the case of how enterprises adopted Microsoft Office. Microsoft developed Office for individual home PC users. But when secretaries and others started bringing Office to the office, installing it on their work computers, a grassroots movement arose. No marketing was involved, just word of mouth, tribe to tribe to tribe. Today, Microsoft Office enjoys more than 90 percent market share among enterprise users.

Other "benign" herd behaviors occur in everyday situations where people make decisions based on the decisions or behavior of others. Suppose you and your spouse are walking down the street in search of a place to eat dinner. Restaurants A and B both look appealing—it's a toss-up— but they're both empty because it's early in the evening. You randomly choose restaurant A. Soon another hungry couple walks down the same street. The two restaurants look about the same to them, too, but when they see that restaurant A has customers, they choose A. As the same thing happens with more passersby, restaurant A ends up doing more business that night than B. This phenomenon is referred to as an "information cascade."

The Tipping Point

"The tipping point is that magic moment when an idea, trend, or social behavior crosses a threshold, tips, and spreads like wildfire," writes Malcolm Gladwell in his book *The Tipping Point*. He observes that change often occurs quickly and counterintuitively and that "little differences" can sometimes impact big changes. As with epidemics, the

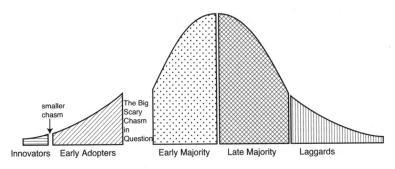

Figure 9.1 A Model of How Change Occurs in a Market

success or failure of corporate endeavors can spread or die in unpredictable ways, depending on whether the tipping point is reached. Gladwell defines a tipping point as "the moment of critical mass, the threshold, the boiling point."

In his 1991 book *Crossing the Chasm*, Geoffrey Moore identifies not one tipping point but *two* critical points—two "chasms"—that determine whether a change will take place in a market. Moore's model follows the basic law of diffusion of innovation, which when visually represented, looks like a bell curve. Figure 9.1 is based on Moore's model.

Moore's model includes five distinct groups:

Innovators (4 percent)
Early adopters (16 percent)
Early majority (33 percent)
Late majority (33 percent)
Laggards (14 percent)

While Moore's model pertains specifically to markets, individuals in organizations adopt new ideas in a similar fashion. There are always a few people—tribal leaders—who are willing to challenge the status quo within an enterprise. These tribal leaders are like innovators and early adopters within a market. If a tribal leader is successful at bridging the two chasms and then convincing enough people to follow her lead, her movement can reach the tipping point and influence change throughout the whole organization.

Story Leader to Tribal Leader to Tribe

Based on our new understanding of how change occurs within enterprises, we now advise our workshop participants not just to focus on the so-called decision maker but also to find the tribal leaders—the people within an enterprise who (1) are willing to hear your story, (2) believe the status quo is worth changing, and (3) demonstrate a willingness and ability to share that belief with other tribes, to say, "Follow me." The more disruptive (non–status quo) your idea, product, or service, the more resistance you'll get from the majority; a good idea, however, will eventually find its way to the majority and to the so-called decision makers.

Every large organization, enterprise, and social group is made up of smaller tribes. These tribes form around common beliefs, ideas, and values. All tribes have a tribal leader—the individual who believes in connecting his or her tribe with other tribes. Tribal leaders reveal themselves when they begin to connect openly with others. When you successfully influence a tribal leader, it's like dropping a stone into a pond, creating ever-widening ripples on the water; your influence spreads exponentially. Of course, the

Figure 9.2 How Change Spreads Within an Enterprise

pattern of spread within an enterprise isn't as predictable as concentric circles. It might look more like a web or network of webs (see Figure 9.2).

The point is that it takes only one salesperson who influences one tribal leader to start the spread of an idea. In this way, one salesperson can move an entire enterprise.

Mike's Story: Keith's One Guy (Part Two)
Keith didn't have to "start high." All he had to do was start with one tribal leader, who then gave rise to more tribes. Eventually, one of those tribes included a C-level executive—the same one I had contacted the year before—who had the ability to affect a much larger tribe, which in turn led to the tipping point at which IBM moved as a herd. Then the enterprise sale was made.

In Keith's case, he ended up with a multimillion-dollar sale. IBM purchased the licensing to Solution Selling, which it then privately branded as its own Signature Selling model and used to train more than 15,000 IBM salespeople. To this day, when I'm at an IBM office, there are still people who ask me to autograph their copy of *Solution Selling*.

Keith went on to make other large enterprise sales by intuitively understanding tribal and herd behavior. It wasn't that he thought selling high was ineffective. He knew it was a way, just not the *only* way. He didn't worry about influencing the person with "budget" but focused instead on finding a "VP of change"—a person who knew how to advance an idea within his or her enterprise.

Help Your Tribal Leader Become a Story Leader

We believe the most powerful tool to influence a tribal leader is stories. Stories are the most effective means by which we communicate our values and beliefs and influence others to believe what we believe, and beliefs and values are what connect tribes. Stories can provide the vehicle by which ideas can be spread from tribe to tribe, leading to movements. Even if you succeed in making contact at the C level, the executive won't necessarily perceive a need for change unless those around her seek to change the status quo. So don't get focused solely on access to the person with "budget." Ask yourself, *Is she in the tribe? Is she a tribal leader?* Think of yourself as a "story leader" who focuses on starting a grassroots internal movement by getting a tribal leader and his or her tribe of similarly minded people excited about a new idea, belief, or message.

In fact, when a seller overtly seeks, through a lower-level executive, access to the decision maker or the person who signs off on deals, the seller risks demotivating the lower-level executive from becoming a tribal leader. *If I'm just a stepping stone for this guy,* the lower-level exec thinks to himself, *why should I bother being his champion?* We can only imagine how many deals salespeople have lost over the years because of our poor understanding of how change actually occurs in an enterprise.

Ultimately, the level in the enterprise at which you need to connect depends on several variables—for example, the size of the potential transaction, the level of disruption your offering poses to the organization, and the number of people affected. And, yes, buy-in from a C-level executive can be a requirement for some sales; however, the C-level executive is just one person. Keep in mind that the C-level executive is more likely to move once the organization around her has already sensed the need to change. If that's the case, it's likely tribes are already connected to the new idea and are in discussions with other potential vendors.

Helping Your "One" Become a Tribal Leader

Create the ripples, starting with one person who's willing to listen to your story and wants to challenge the status quo. Then empower that person to tell his or her own story within the tribe. In order to do this, tend to and document your prospect's story.

Imagine you've just had an ideal sales call. You totally connected with your prospect. Now you need that person to become a tribal leader and start selling for you. But how can you teach a prospect to tell her story in a 45-minute sales call? The answer is, you can't. After all, you've probably been perfecting your own story for weeks or even months. The question, then, is what *can* you do?

First, make sure you have a powerful story. A story that moves a listener emotionally is more likely to be remembered and retold—and more likely to be internalized and adopted by your prospect.

Second, close your call by telling your prospect that you'd like to send her an e-mail summing up your conversation in order to make sure you "got" who she is and that you're both on the same page.

Third, help your tribal leader effectively build her own story by documenting it in an e-mail. As mentioned in Chapter 8, reflection is an essential part of story tending, as it ensures that the listener "gets" the whole story accurately and completely. Be sure that the story includes all the essential elements mentioned in Chapter 5:

○ **Point**. Your prospect's belief, mission, or goal around which the tribe will form.
○ **Setting**. How your prospect's journey started, the character(s), and the emotions.
○ **Complication**. Your prospect's challenges and pains along the way, including the impact of those pains and the emotions involved.
○ **Turning point**. Focus on the timing. Why take action now?
○ **Resolution**. The resolution to your prospect's story takes place in the future, when the enterprise will use your offering to address its challenges.

Here is an example of how to document a prospect's story after a call with a vice president of sales.

From: Ben Zoldan <Ben@storyleaders.com>
Sent: Weds, 19 May 2010 03:00:24
To: Beth <Beth@enterprise.com>
Subject: Discussion Summary

Dear Beth,

It was great talking with you today. Thanks for sharing with me your beliefs, the challenges you're facing, and your goals. I'm writing because I want to make sure I fully understand your story. I'd like to start with a recap of our conversation.

As with many sales managers, you told me you find yourself in a situation where the majority of your sales are being generated by a select few salespeople. You indicated that you believe the bottom 80 percent of your salespeople, given the proper training and tools, are capable of doing much better, and that their improved performance will have a significant impact on your company's success.

> The Point

Your belief in the potential of your salespeople is based on experience. After fifteen years in sales—starting as a frontline salesperson and culminating with your elevation to sales manager six years ago—you recognize that the members of your sales force have the expertise, intelligence, dedication, and drive necessary to succeed.

> Setting

What's missing is something else. As we talked about your best salespeople—the three who accounted for almost 90 percent of your sales last year—you said that what sets them apart is the rare ability to connect, on a human level, with their customers, generating trust and enthusiasm. On the contrary, the rest of your salespeople have weaker interpersonal skills. "As smart as they are," you said, "they have a tough time connecting."

> Complication

181

Up until now, executives in your organization weren't particularly concerned about the distribution of sales so long as the department was meeting its goals. Recently, however, they've acknowledged that the situation puts (Turning Point) the company at risk. The loss of a single top seller could wreck your numbers. Not only are they now eager to address the issue, but they'd like to do so before the end of the year.

In discussing possible solutions, we talked about the fact that what the best sellers do—connecting with people—isn't an innate ability that you either have or you don't. On the contrary, given proper models and (Resolution) training, it's something *all* salespeople can learn to do— to connect through stories, to listen empathetically. We also talked about the value of building a culture around the stories of a company.

You suggested we get together to further discuss the Story Leaders approach. Before we schedule a meeting, would you mind letting me know if I understand your situation?

I'm looking forward to continuing our conversation.

Sincerely,

Ben

We've found that such an e-mail is of great value in an enterprise sales cycle for several reasons:

○ It reflects the story in a way that ensures that you "got" the prospect; if you didn't, the prospect can easily reply with revisions, editing the story.

- It provides your prospect with a written version of the story; you are essentially coaching that person in how to tell the story.
- An e-mail is easily forwarded to other potential tribe members, who in turn are better able to tell the story themselves if they have it in writing for reference. This has proven to be the number-one use of e-mail in the sales cycle. Good letters that tell a story get forwarded, especially upstairs to higher-level tribes. An e-mail provides a safe way for a tribal leader to communicate to a higher-level tribal leader and creates the ripple effect.
- Writing the story yourself gives you the opportunity to anticipate and address questions or concerns that other tribal leaders may have about your offering. They can edit the letter and/or ask for clarification in writing.
- An e-mail can be used for internal documentation inside your organization—for management to qualify for use of resources, for facilitating co-selling by support staff, for application engineers to demonstrate or "present" the product at a later date, and so on.
- As an e-mail circulates, it can also facilitate spread by word of mouth.

Connected or Unconnected?

Your prospect's reply to your e-mail message will help give you a sense of his or her level of enthusiasm for your offering and a sense of how strongly the two of you connected, a critical first step in the seller-buyer relationship. Consider two possible responses to the previous letter.

Response 1

------ Forwarded Message
From: Beth <Beth@enterprise.com>
Sent: Thurs, 20 May 2010 01:00:54
To: Ben Zoldan <Ben@storyleaders.com>
Subject: RE: Discussion Summary

Ben,

Thanks for the call. We will review your material when time permits. At this point, I cannot attend one of your workshops.

Thank you again for your time and the information.

Best regards,

Beth

Response 2

------ Forwarded Message
From: Beth <Beth@enterprise.com>
Sent: Thurs, 20 May 2010 01:00:54
To: Ben Zoldan <Ben@storyleaders.com>
Subject: RE: Discussion Summary

Hi Ben,

I would love to learn more about your approach and further discuss. Your summary is right on the money—I agree about the power of story as a way to communicate. I once heard that people remember stories 10 times more than they do facts or statistics. I am a big believer in sharing stories as a way to connect with people. It's what I've always known to do. What are you thinking is next?

Beth

Note not only the difference in content but also the difference in tone. The word choice in response 1 is polite but formal—a standard reply—whereas the word choice in response 2 ("I would *love* to learn more. . . . I am a *big believer*. . . .") conveys real emotional connectedness with the seller and offering. If you were Ben's sales manager, which opportunity would you want to invest company resources in?

Consider the story ladder for a complex B2B sale, a "committee" sale in which your solution or offering will impact multiple silos—for example, engineering, production, operations, finance, order processing, sales, marketing—within your prospect's organization. Each silo is a tribe. As an insider, your tribe leader will know far more than you ever could about the internal politics and personal agendas at play within the enterprise. Your tribal leader will also be in a much better position to identify other tribal leaders who might embrace your story.

The more complex the organizational decision-making process, the more important it will be for you to follow "interdepartmental bread crumbs" when you are tending your tribal leader's story. If you know your tribal leader will have to get other silos on board, build into your reflected story complications and benefits that pertain to other silos. Give the story the broadest possible appeal. And remember: stories are our most powerful way to create movements and motivate prospects to influence change within their organizations. Find your tribal leaders and help them lead change.

CHAPTER 10

The "Storiable" Organization

[
I think the most important thing about coaching is that you have to have a great sense of confidence about what you're doing. You have to be a salesman, and you have to get your players, particularly your leaders, to believe in what you're trying to accomplish.

—Phil Jackson
]

Helping to Make Great Salespeople

Salespeople can't do it alone. In order to become great sellers, they need the support of their organizations, from CEOs and marketing departments down to the sales managers on the front lines. That's who this chapter is for: CEOs, product marketers/product trainers, and sales managers—the people who exert the strongest influence over an organization's salespeople. We'll address each group's role individually.

Up until now, this book has focused on influencing change in buyers by using stories to forge emotional connections and make points. But buyers aren't the only people a leader needs to influence. As a CEO, marketer, or sales manager, you can influence your salespeople to believe what you believe, to "buy in" to your values, your beliefs, your mission, your company, and your products. Think of sales reps as internal customers. If you can effectively influence them to believe, they will in turn influence their customers to believe.

Part One: CEOs

Let's start with CEOs. As the highest ranking corporate officers, CEOs are uniquely positioned to influence salespeople and their performance. In the following section, we'll discuss ways in which CEOs can enable salespeople to be their best.

The CEO's Story

Just as every person has stories to tell, every organization has stories, too. Whether these stories are known and shared throughout the organization—whether there is a "culture of story"—can have a big impact on an organization's internal sense of identity, its public image, and its bottom-line success.

Often a business's stories originate with the founder or top executive. "CEOs are the chief storytellers," says Gerhard Gschwandtner, publisher of *Selling Power* magazine. "If they tell their stories well, and speak in an authentic voice, their stories become the DNA of their business."

Herb Kelleher and Southwest Airlines

No top executive has demonstrated the power of being chief storyteller better than Herb Kelleher, cofounder and former CEO of Southwest Airlines. In the 1960s, air travel in the

United States was expensive as a result of the hub-and-spoke system, and carriers generally offered poor customer service. Kelleher believed there had to be a better way. In 1967, he came up with the idea of an efficient, reliable, low-cost airline that treats its customers well. Over drinks at St. Anthony's Club in San Antonio, Texas, Kelleher and a colleague sketched the airline's first flight route on a cocktail napkin—the now-famous triangle drawing, with three points representing direct flights between Dallas, Houston, and San Antonio.

When Kelleher tried to get his airline off the ground, his efforts were met by lawsuits from other carriers that were threatened by anyone who dared to think outside the box. Despite these legal challenges, Southwest Airlines was launched in 1971 with four planes and three destinations in Texas.

Recognizing that all employees—from pilots to ticketing agents to baggage handlers—contributed to the Southwest customer experience, Kelleher adopted a simple formula: Hire people with personality, share his beliefs with them, and train them well. Make sure all Southwest employees have the information they need to make decisions. Encourage and promote a fun and family-friendly environment for employees, who will in turn treat customers well.

As Kelleher put it, "We tell our people, 'Don't worry about profit. Think about customer service. Profit is a by-product of customer service. It's not an end in and of itself.'"

Kelleher also understood that the most effective way to communicate a set of beliefs and values is through a story. He made sure that every new Southwest employee, at every level—from pilots and flight attendants to baggage clerks—learned the story of why he founded the company. In building a culture around this story at Southwest—in making it the DNA of his business—Kelleher achieved several things.

First, because all Southwest employees know the company's story, they're more likely to embrace the values and beliefs reflected in that story. If you've flown on Southwest, you've seen it for yourself: Southwest employees treat customers well; they seem to enjoy what they do; and they seem to have a genuine emotional connection with the company.

Second, Kelleher's story has given Southwest a clear identity among consumers. Company values are reflected in its TV ads, and the company's story has made its way onto flights, where employees are happy to talk about Southwest's history, and customers are served drinks with cocktail napkins that picture the airline's route map. As a result, most Southwest customers actually know the company's story. By comparison, how well do you know the story of Delta, United, or American Airlines?

The bottom-line result: Southwest Airlines has turned a profit for 24 consecutive years and has seen its stock soar 300 percent since 1990. Today, Southwest is the safest airline in the world and ranks number one in the industry for service, on-time performance, and lowest employee turnover rate. Not surprisingly, *Fortune* magazine has also twice ranked Southwest one of the 10 best companies to work for in America.

What's Your Story, CEO?

The same story elements covered in Chapter 5 are reflected in Herb Kelleher's Southwest Airlines story:

○ **Setting.** In the 1960s, air travel was expensive, customer service was mediocre, and the "hub-and-spoke" route system limited the number of direct flights. Enter Herb Kelleher, who envisioned a new model on his cocktail napkin.

- ○ **Complication**. In an effort to maintain the status quo, other airlines sued to keep Kelleher grounded.
- ○ **Turning point**. Overcoming the lawsuits, Kelleher launched his airline with a new routing system, cheaper fares, and a commitment to customer service.
- ○ **Resolution**. Southwest Airlines has turned a profit for 24 consecutive years, is the safest airline in the world, and ranks number one in the industry for service, on-time performance, and lowest employee turnover rate.

Having a company story isn't enough; you also have to share it. During Oracle's thirtieth anniversary celebration, cofounder and CEO Larry Ellison devoted his entire 45-minute keynote address to the Oracle story—why he founded the company, the struggles he faced, the lessons he learned, how the company ended up reinventing itself, plus all of his dumbass moments along the way. When we do workshops for Oracle and show a video of Ellison's talk, participants inevitably come away saying, "Wow, we're an amazing company."

Sharing a company's story can have a powerful impact on its salespeople:

They'll feel a stronger emotional connection to the company.

They'll embrace the beliefs and values reflected in the story.

They'll spread the story within the company, strengthening the tribe.

They'll retell the story to customers.

They'll be inspired by the story and more passionate about their work.

Part Two: Product Marketers/Product Trainers

Now that we've discussed the ways in which CEOs can influence salespeople, let's turn to a second group—the people who are responsible for product training, product marketing, and field messaging.

Marketing to Internal Customers

How salespeople learn about their company's products (product training, product marketing, marketing communications, etc.) has a big impact on how they sell those products. Ideally, enablement efforts not only educate salespeople but also convey a company's values and enthusiasm, influencing salespeople to believe what the organization wants them to believe about the products so they can then sell them in the field. It makes perfect sense: a salesperson who buys in will have much more success influencing his or her customers to buy in as well.

But at a lot of companies, product training is more like an initiation rite than an occasion for enthusiasm and excitement. Salespeople are subjected to hours of presentations in which they're exposed to so much raw information that they walk out of the meetings like zombies. If you've been through it, you know: it's torture. The only thing worse is to do it to customers.

Dan's Story: How We "Enable" Our Salespeople (Part One)

As a senior product marketing executive of a large information technology company, I've become increasingly frustrated with our product launch process, which fails to take advantage of our innovation leadership. It's always the same: We start with a great idea. We innovate. We get senior management excited. We invest an enormous amount of resources.

Our R&D machine develops a cutting-edge product. Then, when the product is ready for launch, it's our turn—time for product marketing to introduce the product to our sales force . . . at which point we promptly suck the life out of it.

At least that's how it feels.

Our role is to train the sales force about new products, give them the message, and prepare them to sell effectively in the field. But you wouldn't know that from the way we go about doing things. Basically what we do is lock the sales force in a room and overload them with garbage: multiple days of intensive product training featuring a parade of experts, each with a 300-slide PowerPoint deck, each slide with 30 bullets and graphs about those bullets. It's all so left brain: facts, features, details, statistics, market analysis, competitive information, positioning, product performance, logistics, demo instructions, and so on. Half the time I feel like I might as well be an accountant.

During one recent "enablement" session, I remember looking out at the salespeople. They were all sitting there with their arms crossed, checking their BlackBerrys, working on their laptops. It was like a bad sales call.

It's the same approach whether we're rolling out a new product or introducing our line to new hires. We've been doing it this way for years, and it never has worked. By the time we're done, very few of our salespeople are excited about the launch. If a few do buy in, we still manage to confuse the hell out of them. They walk out of our launch meeting asking themselves, *What am I going to do with all this information they just shoved my way?*

Not only are they confused; they're also ill-equipped to sell the product effectively. It's little wonder a lot of them approach buyers with a "superseller" attitude: "I have all the answers. Let me show you why you're making a mistake." Our product marketing actually encourages that sort of behavior, because it's exactly what *we* do to our salespeople: "Field, here's the latest, greatest product. We'll tell you everything you need to know. . . ." We get our sellers to cross their arms and disengage, then they go out into the field and do the same thing to customers.

Sal's Story: This Is Enabling?

I'm a senior sales executive at an IT integrator. In January, I went to Austin, Texas, for a two-day enablement session hosted by my vendor partner, who was rolling out a new cloud offering to companies like ours that function as value-added resellers for them. In essence, we're their sales force, and they wanted to train us on this new product.

The session kicked off at 8:30 a.m. after a group breakfast. By 10 a.m., I found myself texting my marketing guy, telling him that we were already on slide number 149 and the day had hardly started. The rest of the morning was more of the same, but I sucked it up because I was excited about a presentation on the new cloud offering that was scheduled for midafternoon. My company was 90 percent done building its own cloud solution, and I'd played a big role in the planning and execution. I was excited to learn more about the cloud market and clarify that we were on the right path.

That's not what happened, though. After lunch, the executive responsible for her organization's cloud offering started her presentation, which involved about 100 slides of market data, technical terms, and abstract concepts. I had no idea what she was talking about or how she wanted my company, as a reseller, to execute. In fact, by the time she was done, I was confused about what *cloud* even meant.

As soon as I got in my car, I called my office to tell them how the day had gone. "These damn PowerPoint presentations," I said. "They just confuse me."

Make the Message "Storiable"

Product training doesn't have to be torture. It's all a matter of how information is presented. "Marketing," writes Seth Godin, "is the orchestration of stories shared through social networks." If you want to enable your sellers, articulate your company's message about a product in storiable terms.

We already know that stories are our most powerful tool to influence buyers to believe what we believe. Product trainers would do well to think of their company's salespeople as internal customers. Sell to them in the same way you would have them sell to customers in the field. Model it for them. Tell them stories, inspire them, get them to open up, and build tribes. They can then retell those stories when it's their turn to sell.

Just as individuals and businesses have stories, so do products. Think about the birth of your product as a journey with an arc: Whose idea was it? What's interesting about that person? What (and whose) need was it designed to address? What were the dumbass moments in the development of the product? What lessons did you learn along the way? How could a customer be helped by the product? Instead of talking about product specs, talk about how a real human being can use it, in specific terms. These are the stories that will get your sellers to buy in. They're also the stories that will enable them to connect with and influence customers in the field. Think about the storiable messages you want in the public domain. Because stories get retold, sellers listening to marketing's stories will pass those along to their customers.

It's the same approach Steve Jobs used so effectively when Apple rolled out a new product such as the iPhone or iPad. He told the product's story and didn't clutter the mind with bullets.

Dan's Story: How We Enable Our Salespeople (Part Two)

In our latest launch, we tried doing things differently. Traditionally, our messaging was all *whats* and *hows*—no *whys* and no stories. We realized that we needed to treat our salespeople as internal customers. We needed to connect with them, inspire them, and influence them to share the stories of our products.

This time, instead of burying them in data from the get-go, we hosted a custom Story Leaders workshop and started by sharing the story of our offering—why and how we developed it, our mistakes and hiccups along the way, and so on. We dropped the Superman act. We connected with our constituents.

The reaction from the salespeople was like night and day. Looking out at the audience, I could tell they were more engaged, buying in. They left the training session motivated and inspired. We succeeded in creating a tribe that has a story it can retell, creating other tribes who'll share a passion for the story of our new product.

PowerPoint Isn't the Problem

In criticizing traditional sales training and enablement presentations, we don't mean to demonize PowerPoint. PowerPoint isn't the problem; it's how we use it.

Product marketers often think their job is to educate salespeople by providing them with information—everything about *how* a product works—but they essentially end up doing what Zoe's teacher did with history. Take one of our clients, for example. They were introducing a product designed to integrate and streamline IT silos. Their tagline was "Making IT Easier." They then proceeded to roll out the product to their salespeople using more than 250 slides of graphs, charts, and bullet lists!

Imagine being a salesperson sitting in such a product meeting. What are you going to do when it's time to go on a sales call? Probably you'll end up regurgitating that same presentation to a prospect, who won't enjoy it any more than you did.

Bullet lists and other text-heavy presentations activate the left brain. When the left brain is overstimulated, it sabotages the participation of the right brain. Visual stimuli can, however, activate the right brain. When we show a slide with text, the listener stops listening and begins to read. An alternative approach is to present slides with visual images that represent ideas. If a slide needs explanation—say, to convey a point to a salesperson who is going to repurpose the presentation—use speaker notes at the bottom for your private reference rather than text that will be visible to the audience. Think of a presentation not as a body of information but as a story. Make a storyboard with the setting, complication, turning point, and resolution. Tell stories throughout your presentation as well.

Author Scott Young discusses the concept of "visceralization" (*visceral* plus *visualization*) in *Learn More, Study Less*: "This is the process of creating a mental image. Visceralization is my word to describe imagining not only a mental picture, but sounds, sensations, and emotions. Often a mental image will work, but connecting an idea to several senses and even emotional states can create a stronger link than a picture."

For example, let's say that during a presentation you want to make the point that most companies' IT departments are in disarray. Instead of showing a bulleted list detailing the problems, you could show a photo of a train wreck while you talk about the problems. Such visual metaphors are more memorable and have more impact than a bulleted list because they evoke a visceral, emotional response.

Presentations can tell stories; so can visuals on slides. Once you start thinking of your presentations as stories, building them can be easy and less "slidey." Use storyboards. Insert visuals that create a visceral, lasting impression of the points you want to make. Use bullet points, lists, and statistics to activate the left brain, but do so sparingly. Use images to activate the right brain. And avoid tedious explanations on the slides, thereby limiting the amount of text for the concepts you plan to cover verbally.

Ben's Story: A Picture Is Worth a Thousand Words

A couple of years ago, my family and I were in New York City having breakfast at a diner on the Upper East Side when I got distracted by a loud conversation at the next table. It was an odd scene. A slightly disheveled-looking older woman was aggressively lecturing two young men in nice suits.

"Look at this picture," she said to the men, pointing to one of several photographs spread across the table. "What do you see? Come on. What do you *see?*"

I admit, I was annoyed—I just wanted to have a peaceful breakfast. At the same time, though, I was intrigued. How did this cranky old lady come to be berating these two Madison Avenue types? I was still trying to get a read on the situation when my wife, an artist, leaned over and whispered to me.

"Don't look now," she said, "but that's Annie Leibovitz."

Annie Leibovitz, as in one of my wife's idols, the most influential American portrait photographer of our time, the last person to photograph John Lennon, the woman whose now-famous portrait of Demi Moore, naked and pregnant, graced the cover of *Vanity Fair*.

At first, I didn't believe it. So I Googled "Leibovitz" on my iPhone. Sure enough, it was her. By now, my wife and I were both listening to the conversation. Leibovitz was pointing to yet another photograph.

"How about this one?" she asked the two men. "What's the *story* here? How does it make you *feel?*"

I often think back to that breakfast when I'm considering how we as humans respond to visual stimuli. Leibovitz clearly understood that emotive images can tell whole stories that we process in the blink of an eye. It's an idea totally in keeping with neuroscience, which tells us that all of our senses are kinesthetically connected to our limbic brains. By studying chemical flows, researchers know that all sensory input is initially processed in the limbic brain, before signals are then sent to various parts of the outer brain. So in the case of a photo, the signal goes directly from our eyes to the limbic brain. The same thing happens when we experience any visual stimuli: the limbic brain says, "I like it" or "I don't like it." It's an emotional decision.

Since that breakfast, I've realized two things. First, PowerPoint slides can be used to convey a scene in a story in the same way a good photographer conveys a story through pictures. Second, an emotive image on a PowerPoint slide can be an effective way of achieving "visceralization." We believe marketing departments should keep in mind the power of emotive images when they "sell" to the field just as salespeople should when making presentations to buyers.

Part Three: Sales Managers

Unlike CEOs and product marketers, sales managers are on the front lines every day, shouldering direct responsibility for their teams. Perhaps no one else exerts a stronger influence on salespeople. In this third section, we'll discuss the role sales management plays in helping sellers succeed.

The Front Line: Managing Sellers to Be Their Best

Most sales managers were once sales representatives themselves—and very good ones. The best typically get promoted to management. Unfortunately, a lot of successful salespeople crash and burn once they become managers. The conventional wisdom says this happens because selling and managing involve different skills, but the conventional wisdom is wrong. Selling and managing are both all about influencing people to change. Just as selling requires getting buyers to open up and believe what you believe, managing requires getting reps to open up and buy into your company's products and sales approach.

So why do so many top sellers make poor managers? It's not the difference in the jobs; it's the difference in the way they approach those jobs. When sellers become managers, a lot of them stop selling. They stop connecting with people and developing the kind of interpersonal relationships that were the foundation of their success in the field. They abandon the very things that got them where they are because they hold the misguided belief that managing calls for something else: control. And so they turn to spreadsheets, plans, forecasts, and expense reports—the province of the left brain.

Ben's Story: We Do What We Know

When I was a rep, I hated weekly sales meetings. My manager would have us come into the office early on Monday mornings so he could ask us about our pipelines, our forecasts, our appointments, our "commits." Basically, it was a watchdog exercise, a total waste of time, and everybody knew it. I think even my manager hated those meetings.

But as soon as I was promoted to management, I did the same thing. I'd call in my reps and interrogate them the same way I'd been interrogated. *What do you have this week? What's on your forecast? What's going to close?* Not surprisingly, I didn't get straight answers. My reps were just like I'd been: their number-one goal was to get me off their backs.

As a manager, I hated those meetings even more than before, but I didn't know a better way. I was doing what I'd been taught. The meetings were all about what we needed to do to "get the deal." We never talked about lessons learned. There was no self-reflection. Being vulnerable wasn't an option. It's little wonder I never really connected with my reps.

Know Your Horses

Interpersonal relationships can be one of the most important parts of a sales manager's job. In order to build a winning team, you've got to "know your horses." Such was the case, literally, with the racehorse Seabiscuit. Seabiscuit's first trainer, James "Sunny Jim" Fitzsimmons, had trained horses for years. Early on, he saw potential in two-year-old Seabiscuit. But under Fitzsimmons, Seabiscuit didn't perform to expectations. "The horse is too lazy," Fitzsimmons said. (Funny, we hear the same thing from sales managers about their lower-performing reps.)

Fitzsimmons's strategy was to break down Seabiscuit and beat the laziness out of him. It didn't work. Seabiscuit finished last or in the back of the pack for his first 10 races. With nothing to lose, Seabiscuit's owners turned to a washed-up old "horse whisperer" named Tom Smith. Tom's unorthodox training methods brought Seabiscuit out of his lethargy. Seabiscuit started winning virtually every race, becoming the number-one racehorse in the country. Same horse, same potential, different result. The only difference was a new trainer ("manager") who put in the time and effort to actually get to know his horse. (By the way, do you think motivation comes from the emotional brain or thinking brain? Hint: Seabiscuit didn't have a thinking brain.)

Or consider the Chicago Bulls between 1984 and 1989. Despite having an amazing young talent in Michael Jordan, as well as future Hall of Famer Scottie Pippen and All-Star Horace Grant, the Bulls weren't anywhere close to being a championship team. It's easy to forget, but before MJ was MJ, he was widely criticized as being selfish, a prolific scorer with unbelievable athletic ability who couldn't and didn't win. In the 1986–1987 season, he led the league in scoring with 37 points per game; however, the Bulls were swept in the first round of the playoffs, just as they had been the previous year. In fact, through Jordan's first six seasons, the Bulls made it past the first round of playoffs only once.

Then everything changed. Phil Jackson replaced Doug Collins as the Bulls' head coach for the 1989–1990 season. Fans had their doubts. An NBA journeyman, Jackson had never been an NBA head coach. "My goal," Jackson told a crowd at Old St. Patrick's Church in Chicago, "is to find a structure that will empower everybody on the team, not just the stars, and allow the players to grow as individuals as they surrender themselves to the group effort."

In addition to changing the Bull's playing strategy and laboriously training them in the triangle offense, Jackson incorporated a holistic approach, asking his players for full commitment to his values and his moral "system," which was influenced by Eastern philosophy (and earned him the nickname "Zen Master"). Keep in mind that Jackson was born to two Christian ministers, so he knew something about communicating his beliefs. He knew how to inspire others to believe what he believed. He employed unconventional coaching methods. Sometimes when he wanted to make a point, he'd have his players watch a movie. He gave homework in the form of reading assignments, novels and essays that he felt fit the personalities of his players. Most of all, he got to know his players—where they were coming from and what made them tick.

The following year, with no major roster changes, the Bulls won the NBA championship. The main difference was Jackson. By 1998, with Jackson at the helm, the Bulls had won six NBA championships, making the playoffs every year and failing to win the title only three times. Jordan was no longer known as a selfish scorer. He had become one of the best defensive players in the league, named First Team All-NBA Defensive Team in each of his eight years under Jackson. How did Jackson change MJ and turn the Bulls around? He got MJ to buy in.

Jackson proved his success in Chicago was no fluke. In 2000, he was hired to coach the Los Angeles Lakers. Despite having two of the game's top stars in Shaquille O'Neal and Kobe Bryant, the Lakers hadn't won a championship in years. As with the young Michael Jordan, O'Neal and Bryant were criticized for not being team players. But once again, with no major roster moves, Jackson was able to guide the Lakers to the championship in his first year as coach. By 2010, the Lakers had five titles.

Jackson retired with 11 titles as head coach, more than any head coach or manager in U.S. professional sports. Sure, he had great players on his teams—MJ, Pippen, Shaq, and Kobe—but they didn't win until Phil came along. His leadership was what made the difference.

How did Jackson do it? "He spent time with his players," said Steve Kerr, who played for three of Jackson's championship teams in Chicago, in a story for *ESPN Magazine*. "He thought about what made them tick. He connected with them, sold them on his concept, stuck up for them when they needed him. His actual coaching—calling plays, working refs, figuring out lineups, and everything else that we see—was a smaller piece of a much bigger picture. His players competed for him for many reasons, but mainly because they truly believed Jackson cared about them. Which he definitely did."

Kobe Bryant, interviewed for the same *ESPN Magazine* story, agreed: "He's absolutely brilliant in bringing a group together to accomplish one common goal."

But let's give the final word to the NBA's greatest player of all time. After his last game with the Bulls, Jordan was asked about playing for another coach. "How many times do you want me to say it?" Jordan replied. "If Phil's not in Chicago, I'm not playing—anywhere."

Leading Is Selling, Selling Is Leading

It's not always easy getting someone to open up, especially salespeople in a corporate setting. A sales manager can be a leader by going first. In Chapter 6 we presented Ben's story about Clear Technology's vice president of sales Phil Godwin, who tried Story Leaders as a last resort to help his sellers. Here's a story from Phil himself.

Phil Godwin's Story: Connecting with My Rep

After the Story Leaders workshop, I started using what I'd learned to connect with clients, and it was working well. But I was having less luck managing some of my reps. Last fall, I started noticing a morale problem with one in particular.

Steve was an average rep who typically followed directions well, but he was starting to get very negative. I could feel him drifting away, not doing the things that he needed to get done. I addressed the problem in my usual way, talking to him, asking questions to find out what the problem was. But in this case, I already had a pretty good idea of what the problem was. Steve wasn't making enough money, and his bills were piling up. On the positive side, his pipeline was full, and he was set to make a lot of money in the next four months. But he was so stressed out he couldn't see the light at the end of the tunnel.

Around the same time, I was having a struggle with my middle son. He'd started fifth grade full of excitement. All his friends were in the same class. They felt like kings of the hill, their last year of elementary school. But a few weeks into the year, things started going downhill. My son's teacher started riding him. He'd always struggled with schoolwork, and her approach was only making him feel worse.

205

Every day was a battle for my son, and every evening was a battle for us, trying to get him to do his homework. He felt that no matter what he did, his teacher was going to tell him it was wrong. In the mornings, he didn't want to get out of bed. "I'm not going back to that place," he'd say. Around the same time, we were having some testing done, and the doctors determined that he had dyslexia. It was exciting to know the root cause of his problems and shift attention to getting him help. We still had the teacher problem, though. I found myself having to explain to a fifth-grade boy that he'd have to be the bigger person when dealing with this adult.

One afternoon, after I'd spent hours on the phone with school administrators, I had another meeting with my struggling rep, Steve, and I couldn't seem to get through to him. *How am I supposed to help this guy if he won't open up?* I thought. And that's when it finally hit me: I'd been using what I learned in the Story Leaders workshop to connect with customers, but it hadn't occurred to me that I could and should be doing the same thing with my people. I hadn't been leading the way I'd been selling. In order to motivate Steve, I needed to connect with him.

And so I told him the story of what I'd been going through with my son, how his teacher had broken his spirit.

"I hear you," Steve said with a laugh. "I know all about being broke."

He then proceeded to tell me about some of his financial problems. By the time he left my office, he was in better spirits. I hadn't solved his problem, but I'd shown that I understood; I'd connected with him. And that was enough. His attitude changed. He went on to close the big deals in his pipeline and ended up having his best year ever. I hate to think what would have happened if I had started "managing" him instead of connecting with him. I learned two things from that experience. First, to get my reps to really open up and let me in, I need to go first and let them into my life. Second, I can draw on my own experiences to tell stories that convey the points I want to make.

Stories Are Our Most Powerful Tool

Remember Ben's story about his therapist Alana in Chapter 3? Ben's mistake as a salesperson was in thinking he had to be perceived as Superman in order to succeed. A lot of sales managers make the same mistake. The result is that they fail to connect emotionally with their salespeople.

Who are your reps? What makes them tick? Where do they come from? Why do they do what they do? In order to influence change in your reps, try opening up and inspiring them with stories of your own lessons learned and how you fumbled along the way. In doing so, not only will you connect with your reps but you'll also be modeling effective selling behaviors and building a culture of story. As Howard Gardner, professor of cognition and education at Harvard University, puts it, "Stories are the single most powerful tool in a leader's toolkit."

But leaders aren't the only people with important stories to tell. Sales reps can learn a lot from each other's stories as well. Firefighters have long understood the value of such peer-to-peer story sharing. Every night, in firehouses across the country, firefighters take part in a tradition where they share stories about their day. It's more than just a social ritual; it's a means by which firefighters learn from one another's successes and failures and build institutional memory within their departments. The goal: to make sure every single member of the firehouse has the same level of situational knowledge. With lives at stake, the 87/13 rule simply is not an option in the firefighting profession.

Sales managers can foster similar peer-to-peer learning by encouraging reps to share stories (including dumbass selling moments) with each other. One of our clients actually replaced his weekly sales meeting with what he calls "The Monday Morning Campfire." Instead of focusing on forecasts and pipelines, he goes around the horn and has each of his team members share a story about a recent selling experience. The young reps learn from the old reps, the old reps learn from the young reps, and because the lessons come through storytelling, they're much more likely to be remembered and taken to heart than anything learned from a sales manual. Since our client implemented the campfire meetings, attendance is up, morale is up, and his salespeople are more engaged. The meetings also promote a culture of story and reinforce the way he wants his sellers to communicate with buyers.

Personal Connection Is What Matters Most

We all like to feel we are part of something bigger than ourselves. None of us wants to feel like a cog in a machine. The company provides the paycheck, but employees work for people. Personal relationships and interactions are much more important than staff meetings or formal performance evaluations. Lead by example. Treat your salespeople the way you want them to treat your customers.

In the end, whether you're a manager, marketer, or CEO, one of the goals is to enable your reps to become better salespeople. As Herb Kelleher demonstrated at Southwest Airlines, if you focus on helping your people become better at what they do, everything else will fall into place.

CHAPTER 11

Continuing the Journey

[
The closer psychologists look at the careers of the gifted, the smaller the role innate talent seems to play and the bigger the role preparation seems to play.
]

—Malcolm Gladwell, *Outliers: The Story of Success*

Part One: Trying It

Give this a try: Set down this book and put your hands together, interlocking your fingers. Now look at your hands. Which thumb is on top? Now put your *other* thumb on top. Feels all wrong, right? That's because you've been doing it the other way your whole life. Trying anything new takes us out of our comfort zone.

This chapter is going to help you try the new things you've learned in this book. They might be uncomfortable at first. Expect to struggle. Don't be afraid to make mistakes.

Ben's Story: John Burke's Guilt

John Burke is the group vice president of Oracle's applications business unit. The first time I ever talked to John was when I cold-called him. We had a pretty good conversation, during which he shared his frustration with the 80/20 rule.

"At Oracle," he said, "It's more like 90/10."

As part of his evaluation of Story Leaders, he wanted to preview the model and agreed to attend one of our public workshops in Del Mar, California. But he had one condition: "If I come out to Del Mar, take me golfing."

"Sure," I said. "We'll play golf."

Later, I learned that John is an avid horse racing fan, too. I didn't realize that the area's great golf courses—and Del Mar's racetrack—were probably the main reasons he agreed to come at all.

The workshop lasted two-and-a-half days, so I scheduled a tee time at nearby La Costa Resort for the afternoon of the third day. I'd been monitoring John for his buy-in during the workshop, but I decided that asking him about it over golf would be too salesy. By the sixteenth hole, though, I couldn't help myself.

"So, what do you think, John? Do you see Story Leaders helping?"

John was brutally honest. "I get it, I really do," he said. "But I don't know if Oracle is ready for it. It's different than what we do, and quite frankly, it feels a little weird. Plus the name, Story Leaders—that's weird, too. Probably too weird for us."

I thought about all the time I had spent with him and the money I'd just spent on the round of golf and proceeded to hit my next ball into a water hazard. I didn't regain my composure until we got to the last hole.

"How about this?" I said. "I know it feels weird now, but since I took you golfing, do me a favor. On your next sales call, try everything you learned in the workshop. Start with, 'Can I tell you a story?' End by passing the torch. And play back what the prospect tells you. Tend his story."

I knew I was playing on John's guilt, but I didn't see another way.

"Okay," he said. "I promise I'll do it on my next sales call."

The following Tuesday, I got a call from John. "My story wasn't very good," he said, "but it worked."

He told me that he and another Oracle executive had just come back from a sales call with the CIO of a Fortune 100 company. Before the meeting, in their prep conversation, John had told his colleague that he wanted to open the sales call with a story—his Who I Represent story from the workshop. But his colleague wasn't comfortable with the story, especially revealing the company's dumbass moment.

"John, you can't say that to a customer," he said. "We don't air our dirty laundry like that."

That only gave John even more incentive to tell the story during the meeting.

"So I started the sales call with the story," John told me on the phone. "The CIO said, 'Thanks, I never hear anything like that from vendors.' And then he tells me *his* story, which included his dumbass moments. It was like a role-play straight from the workshop."

But there was more: "As soon as the meeting was over and we got back into the car, my once-skeptical colleague turns to me and says, 'Tell me that story again. I want to use it.'"

Even though it felt weird for John, using what he'd learned in the workshop and getting real-life feedback from a buyer was the turning point for him. He has since put his whole team through the Story Leaders workshops.

"We've been trained our whole careers to ask diagnostic questions, to deliver value props, to do ROIs. We expect people to respond to all this left-brain stuff, and it usually doesn't work. It turns people off," John says. "Connecting with someone's emotional brain through honest, authentic stories, combined with real listening, is a better way. All the best salespeople I've ever known and all the best sales calls I've ever been on prove this to be true."

The point of the story is, take a chance. Tell your stories. They don't need to be perfect. It will feel weird at first, but don't be afraid to try a new way.

John Burke's Story: Who I Represent

In 2005, when Oracle bought PeopleSoft, we told the world we would "fuse" the two systems, bringing together the best features of both Oracle EBS and PeopleSoft's products. We would call the new system "Fusion."

Right away, an interesting thing happened. Sales slowed down for both product lines. Basically our customers told us, "Look, we've invested a lot to run our business on either PeopleSoft or Oracle EBS. We need you to continue to support our product line."

At first we didn't get it. Our strategy was to take the best from each system and create something better. But we missed something that was critical to our customers at the time. They already had major investments in the systems they had been running, and creating something new would disrupt their environments. Fusing the systems together to make something new and "better" could actually cause problems. That was our dumbass moment: thinking we knew what was best for our customers instead of letting *them* tell *us*.

Fortunately, our customers spoke loud and clear: "If you want to build a new product, we suggest you focus on what has changed and build that rather than your previous idea of merging two systems together."

We listened. Although we thought we were doing the right thing after the merger, within five months of the acquisition, we changed our strategy and announced "Applications Unlimited." Because our customers needed us to support whichever system they had been running, we guaranteed we would continue to build new capabilities for each existing product for five years and that we would provide lifetime support for both systems. As long as a customer wanted to use a product, we would support it.

Our customers were a little skeptical at first, but we delivered with the new releases of PeopleSoft, EBS, and other products. Once we proved we were executing on our commitment, our customers began to do more with us.

Specifically, our customers wanted three things. First, they said they were ready for the cloud, and they wanted software designed to run either in the cloud, in their data centers, or both. Second, they wanted embedded business intelligence, a system that automatically delivered reports and allowed them to view the data however they wanted without having to move it to a warehouse. Third, they wanted built-in collaboration—a way to collaborate among employees, customers, suppliers, and partners built right into the transaction flow of the system.

So those became the driving tenets of our Fusion Applications project.

The point is, we got our original strategy and communication all wrong, but we listened to our customers, and we changed. It has taught us a major lesson in how we listen to our clients, especially during and after acquisitions.

Mike's Story: The Learning Zone

In the late 1980s, a career trainer friend of mine said, "Mike, I have a gift for you, trainer to trainer."

His gift was a diagram of the "learning zone" (see Figure 11.1). He drew three concentric circles on the whiteboard. The middle circle, the "bull's-eye," was the comfort zone, the "I am" zone. The next circle was the learning zone, the "I can" zone. The outer ring was the panic zone, the "I can't" zone.

Today, we share the learning-zone diagram with workshop attendees to help them visualize the idea of change. We then ask them to name the kinds of lessons they've taken. We get answers such as golf lessons, scuba-diving lessons,

Figure 11.1 The Learning Zone

skydiving lessons, piano lessons, and French lessons. Then we ask how comfortable they were the first time they swung a golf club, breathed underwater, jumped out of an airplane, played a scale, or ordered a meal in French. The answer is always the same: "very uncomfortable."

That discomfort is a natural part of learning a new skill. In order to get comfortable doing anything new, you must leave your comfort zone and have the courage to venture into your learning zone.

Part Two: Practice

Mike's Story: Freedom

High school was a difficult time for me. I was small, skinny, and poor. There was no such thing as an allowance in our house. Worse, I had a violent, alcoholic father. From the age of 14 on, I worked seven days a week stocking a retail liquor store. I was saving for a car. To me, driving meant freedom. The day I turned 15 and a half, I was the first person in line at the DMV with my mother to get my learner's permit.

I bought a car that didn't run. My grandfather was a GM mechanic. He patiently showed me how to do everything the car needed. We put in a new clutch, cleaned the carburetor, replaced the points and plugs—the whole deal.

For the six months between getting my learner's permit and taking my driving test, my biggest obstacle was learning to drive a stick shift well enough to start on a hill and parallel park. Talk about something nonintuitive! I was amazed by experienced drivers who effortlessly coordinated the gas, clutch, and gearshift. They could even drive while they were talking and eating. How did they do it?

On my sixteenth birthday, February 1, 1963, in the pouring rain, I was back in line at the DMV with my mother to take the test for my driver's license. Unfortunately, I still hadn't gotten the hang of driving a stick. I had to think through every move I made. It was all very left-brain. During the test, I was concentrating so hard that I failed to hear the fire engine behind me and didn't pull over as I was supposed to. I was mortified, not to mention devastated to think I wasn't going to get my license.

But the DMV examiner took pity on me. Perhaps it was my vulnerability.

"Let's continue," he said.

I nailed the parallel parking, and he passed me. I was getting my driver's license after all. Freedom! It's still one of the biggest days of my life.

Weeks later, I was driving home from my job at the liquor store when I realized I wasn't even thinking about the clutch and gas and gearshift. Driving a stick had become routine. It was all a matter of practice, putting in enough hours.

Letting the Right Brain In

When it comes to learning a new skill, the procedural left brain is in charge. It's focused on the mental bulleted list of tasks that need to be completed to execute the job at hand. In Mike's case, he wasn't able to hear the fire truck because he was concentrating so hard on the mechanics of manipulating the clutch, gas, and gearshift.

But eventually, even activities that are daunting at first—such as driving a stick—become routine. Eventually, we're able to listen to music, have a conversation with a passenger, maintain a broader awareness of road and traffic conditions. It's all a matter of putting in enough practice for the left brain to get the skill down and make it second nature. Only then, once a new skill becomes old hat, can the left brain relinquish some control and let the right brain engage more fully in the activity.

That's the point you're aiming for with your stories. Once you've practiced enough, you won't have to consciously think about the card system, or emoting, or passing the torch. It will all come naturally, allowing you to be fully present with your whole brain instead of self-consciously worrying about each step along the way.

What Happens After You Read This Book?

In *Outliers: The Story of Success*, Malcolm Gladwell examines what makes high achievers different. His conclusion? Practice. About 10,000 hours worth, to be specific.

Here's Gladwell in a *Reader's Digest* interview:

An innate gift and a certain amount of intelligence are important, but what really pays is ordinary experience. Bill Gates is successful largely because he had the good fortune to attend a school that gave him the opportunity to spend an enormous amount of time programming computers—more than 10,000 hours, in fact, before he ever started his own company. He was also born at a time when that experience was extremely rare, which set him apart. The Beatles had a musical gift, but what made them the Beatles was a random invitation to play in Hamburg, Germany, where they performed live as much as five hours a night, seven days a week. That early opportunity for practice made them shine. Talented? Absolutely. But they also simply put in more hours than anyone else.

So how does a kid become the next Bill Gates or Tiger Woods? Gladwell goes on to say that people who become high achievers usually have parents who allow their children to concentrate on and spend extraordinary amounts of time on the activity that makes them happiest and in which they excel. Gladwell suggests that the amount of time high achievers need to invest appears to be 10,000 hours.

Exercises

Fortunately, because human beings are wired to think and learn in story, you won't need to practice 10,000 hours of storytelling in order to influence change in buyers. But you'll still need to practice a lot.

We offer the following exercises to help you develop the skills covered in the preceding chapters:

1. Build your story ladder.
2. Build your Who I Am story.
3. Build your Who I Represent story.
4. Build your Who I've Helped story.
5. Tend a story.
6. Story sharing.
7. Identify a stalled opportunity in your pipeline, and build a story to unstall it.
8. Share your stories with others: www.storyleaders.com/shareyourstory

The exercises are presented in the same order we use them in the workshop, which is itself the basis for the structure of this book. Feel free to skip around as needed.

Quick Story-Building Guide Several of the exercises will prompt you to build stories. In the following paragraphs you'll find a quick refresher on story building.

Before you get started, go to www.storyleaders.com/downloads to download templates. We recommend you keep the storyboard template in front of you while you work, to keep on track.

You should also purchase three-by-five-inch colored index cards at your local office supply or stationery store. You'll need five colors: white, yellow, red, blue, and green. Remember, you should be writing bullet points and keywords on your cards, not complete sentences. Writing complete sentences will activate your left-brain language center and interfere with your right-brain "multichannel" brainstorming. The storyboard is intended to help you organize your ideas. Think of your cards as prompts, not scripts.

1. **The yellow card (your point).** Start by figuring out the point you want to make.
2. **The red card (resolution).** Next, identify the end of your story.
3. **The green card (setting).** Working backwards, decide where your story should start. How did the journey begin?
4. **The white card (complication).** Now that you have the pillars of your story in place (point, resolution, and setting), it's time to describe the struggle, the bumps in the road, the dumbass moments.
5. **The blue card (turning point).** How did things change? Was there an aha moment?

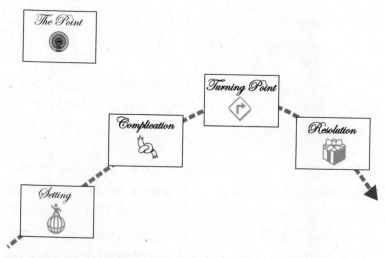

Figure 11.2 The Elements of Your Story Follow an Arc of Change

You now have the elements of a story that follows the arc of change (see Figure 11.2).

6. **Emotions.** On each card (excluding the yellow card), write at least one word that captures the emotion associated with that part of the story. Circle the word(s).

7. **Tell the story.** Use your cards for reference. Start by practicing in front of a mirror; then try it out on someone other than a client. At first, focus on what happened. Once you've got the sequence of events down pat, concentrate on the circled emotion words at the bottom of each card and emote them using nonverbal cues. Don't try to tell the story from memory, without the cards, until it feels like second nature.

Exercise 1: Build Your Story Ladder Create a story ladder for your customers' buy cycle. Start with a blank story ladder like the one in Figure 11.3. Next, make a list of the steps that your

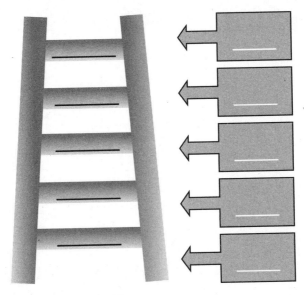

Figure 11.3 Blank Story Ladder

customers go through in their buy cycle. Condense the list into sales stages, and compare it to your current sales process. If they're out of sync, now is a good time to adjust. The stages will be your rungs. Add them to your ladder, starting with the bottom rung and working up to the top rung—your buyer's yes. Now, on the right side of the ladder, indicate which story you'll use for each rung (i.e., the story that will make the point needed to move your buyer up to the next rung).

Exercise 2: Build Your Who I Am Story Your Who I Am story chronicles your professional journey. You're the main character. The point (yellow card) is why you do what you do. The resolution (red card) is your current professional position. Once you identify your point and resolution, chances are that a natural beginning—how your journey began (green card)—will present itself to you. The complications (white card) detail your struggle, bumps in the road, and dumbass moments. The turning point (blue card) chronicles the transformation (possibly an aha moment) when you decided to become who you are today. What led you to change direction or alter your behavior?

A good Who I Am story inevitably shows vulnerability. It requires self-reflection and, often, an admission that there was once a time you weren't as qualified, committed, or capable as you are today.

Exercise 3: Build Your Who (or What) I Represent Story If you work for a company, your Who I Represent story is the company's story. If you're self-employed, your Who I Am and Who I Represent stories are one in the same.

In the story of your company's journey, the main character might be the founder or CEO. If you work for a big company with a broad range of product offerings, consider focusing your story on your particular business unit or product. For instance, instead of building a story about your employer, XYZ Company, which offers thousands of products, focus on the ABC product group you represent. Just as every person has more than one story, so does every company. Resist the urge to try to give a comprehensive company history. Instead, build a manageable story that conveys the point you want to make. That's what John Burke did in his Who I Represent story, presented earlier in this chapter. Instead of trying to tell the whole Oracle story, he focused on a chapter in the company's history that conveyed the point he wanted to make about the importance of listening to your customers and being willing to change.

The point (yellow card) of your Who I Represent story is to show why your company does what it does, including any guiding beliefs or values. The conclusion (red card) is what the company does today. The beginning (green card) is how the journey began. The complications (white card) include challenges the company faced, missteps, and dumb-ass moments. To keep a human face on the story, focus on the complications via the main character's point of view. The turning point (blue card) is the moment at which the company turned itself around or took a new direction that led to what the company does today.

Exercise 4: Build Your Who I've Helped Story You'll want to have at least one Who I've Helped story in your repertoire and probably more. Your customers and clients are the main characters in these stories, which are not about their companies but about their particular, personal journeys and transformations—ideally, transformations that occur because of your offering, product, service, or support. You might be a character in these stories too, perhaps coming onto the scene at the turning point. Your customers and clients can help you build these stories.

The point (yellow card) of a Who I've Helped story is your client's belief—possibly a belief you influenced. The resolution (red card) is what your client is able to do today because of your product or offering. The beginning (green card) is how your client's journey started. Take time to develop your client as a character; a listener will care more about a character who seems like a real person. The complication (white card) details your client's struggles when he did things the "old way." The turning point (blue card) is the aha moment when he started doing things the new way—with your help.

223

If you're fortunate enough to build the story with your client's input, ask him for at least one word that represents the emotion he felt during each part of the story, then write and circle those words on your index cards. When you practice the story, start by telling it to the client, who can correct any mistakes and help you flesh out the narrative.

Exercise 5: Tend to a Personal Story The goal of this exercise is to make another person feel "felt" using empathetic listening skills: awareness, encouragement, and reflection.

Begin by telling a friend, family member, or close colleague a story about your day, then pass the torch with some variation of "enough about my day; how was yours?"

Once your friend starts talking, give her your undivided attention. Use both nonverbal encouragement (voicing "hmm," maintaining eye contact, leaning forward, etc.) and verbal encouragement (e.g., "And?" "Then what?"). If she says something you don't understand, ask for clarification ("Why?" "Can you go back to _____?" "I didn't get what you meant by _____.").

Be aware of nonverbal cues to determine if she's telling you anything she's not actually saying, and follow the bread crumbs. Focus on the emotion behind the words: "Sounds like you're feeling _____, or is it something else?" "Why did you feel that way?" "Where is that coming from?"

When your friend is done, reflect what she told you by summarizing the story in your own words and asking, "Do I get you?" Finally, demonstrate an emotional connection to what you've heard: "When you told me _____, it made me feel _____."

Exercise 6: Story Sharing on a Sales Call The goal of this exercise is to form an emotional connection with a new prospect.

Before you tell a story, soothe your prospect's left brain by letting him know you have a plan for the meeting. For example: "What I'd like to do today is share my story with you and hear yours. Then we can ask each other questions to see if there's a mutual opportunity." Next, activate the prospect's right brain with a brief story (of two to three minutes duration) from your inventory. When you're done, pass the torch (e.g., "Enough about me. So, what's your story?") and tend to his story using empathetic listening skills. When your prospect is done, reflect what he told you by summarizing the story in your own words and asking, "Do I get you?" Figure 11.4 illustrates the give-and-take of storytelling and story sharing.

Prepare to be amazed.

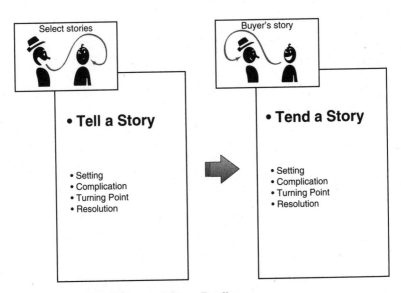

Figure 11.4 Storytelling and Story Tending

Exercise 7: Getting Unstalled Remember Adam's story in Chapter 6 about the dangers of going it alone? The goal of this exercise is to identify a stalled opportunity in your pipeline and build a story to unstall it—the right tool for the job.

Start by brainstorming the reason(s) you believe the opportunity is stalled. What would your buyer need to believe in order to get unstalled? For example, maybe your buyer needs to realize that the cost of not doing anything is greater than the cost of doing something. Your job is to build a story that conveys that belief. Draw on a personal experience in which your failure to act ended up costing you big time.

Use the story to move your buyer up to the next rung of the story ladder (see Figure 11.5).

Exercise 8: Share Your Stories We've created a forum for readers to share stories and read other people's stories at our website: www.storyleaders.com/shareyourstory. We're especially interested in stories about how you used what you've learned in this book.

ddress a Stalled Opportunity in Your Pipeline by Building a
Move Your Buyer Up to the Next Rung of the Story Ladder

Now Get to Work!

By picking up and reading this book, by getting this far, you've demonstrated the desire to try something new. In other words, you're on a journey, traveling the arc of change. You're on your way to a story.

Expect to struggle. Expect complications. In your efforts to become a Story Leader, you'll no doubt have a few dumbass moments along the way. But don't be discouraged. Keep practicing. And remember, we're all natural-born storytellers, even if some of us have gotten a little rusty.

Your turning point will come when you begin to see that the techniques in this book really work. You'll know the moment: *Aha*!

And then there will be a resolution to your struggles. You'll reach the high level of connection that fosters a collaborative, reciprocal sharing of ideas and beliefs—the type of communication that moves people to change.

The ability to influence others to believe what we believe isn't limited to the very few. We can all do it. What we have discussed in this book is an approach that will let you see yourself—really see yourself—drawing upon the meaningful events of your life and sharing them with others. This is the fundamental way we connect with other people. And this connection is the basis for how people allow themselves to be influenced to change. It's no longer a mystery: the ability to make these connections is what makes great salespeople great. It cannot be seen, but it is felt. You just have to take the leap and try it.

The rewards are fantastic.

INDEX

ABOUT THE AUTHORS

Michael Bosworth and **Ben Zoldan** have been collaborators for more than a decade, training tens of thousands of salespeople. They cofounded Story Leaders, LLC, a training firm focused on improving the performance of salespeople. Previously, Michael founded two of the most successful firms in the sales-training industry: Solution Selling and CustomerCentric Selling. Ben has worked in the sales industry for nearly 20 years. Prior to joining Mike as a principal consultant with CustomerCentric Selling, Ben was a top-performing salesperson and a senior sales executive.

Learn more at www.storyleaders.com.